WILL
EVERYONE
BE
SAVED

WILL
EVERYONE
BE
SAVED

KEVIN CARMODY

DEDICATION

I would not have been able to write this book without the inspiration and encouragement of my Savior, Jesus Christ. He gets all the credit for this labor of love. I also thank my wife, Tammii, for showing me, by her boundless love and patience, true friendship. She is a living example of what it means to be a servant of His.

To my children and grandchildren, there is no greater joy I could have as a father and papa than to see you loving Jesus and others the way you do. How blessed I am because of you!

To Chuck and Linda, thank you for introducing me to our Savior. You invited me into your home and showed me the reality of His love. You have made an eternal difference in my life for which I will always be grateful.

CONTENTS

ENDORSEMENTS

"All exhortations to consider the truth of God must have the singular, underlying motive of redemption. With this book, Kevin Carmody speaks with an uncompromising prophetic voice to both believers and seekers of truth, born of his love for people. Grounded in scripture and formed in the crucible of personal experience, "Will Everyone Be Saved" provides clear answers for those wanting to know the truth of God's salvation for mankind."

- Mark Moore
Global Impact Coordinator, City Harvest Church

"Kevin Carmody has a message that is a wake-up call for those who have watered down the gospel of Jesus. It is evident through his amazing personal testimony and thorough research of the bible. As a close friend for many years, Kevin has shown himself to be a man of truth through his words and deeds. He and his wife Tammii have been living testimonies of committed and sacrificial following of Jesus by giving up a comfortable life in America to spread the good news of eternal salvation to those who have not heard. They have lived in warzones and among foreign and neglected peoples to bring them true life and hope because of their love for Jesus and the true meaning of the gospel."

- Dr. Juergen Kramer
Director, All Nations Germany

"This book is a must read for anyone who desires truth and is willing to seek it out. Kevin, who happens to be my father, insightfully explores difficult questions to help the reader understand about their eternal future.

What he presents is solidly grounded in truth and compassion. I can honestly say, regardless of family bias, that what my dad has written will help you find the answer to the paramount question of our time asked in the title of this book."

- Bobby Carmody
Community Pastor, Heart of the City Church

"My friend Kevin Carmody has carried a great burden for many years concerning the attempt to dilute the gospel because of our sentimental bent wanting no one to suffer the eternal wrath of God. Kevin understands that compassion, and he has responded to that deep concern for the human race by dedicating his life to preach this message to the nations and those who have not heard. It is the reality of God's offer of an eternal relationship with Him through His Son Jesus Christ and the reality of eternal separation and suffering for those who reject this offer that has caused Kevin to commit his life to the cause of The Great Commission and to write this book."

- Bob MacGregor
Lead Pastor, City Harvest Church

INTRODUCTION

Contrary to world opinion, God does exist. He does exist and is knowable. So is your eternal destiny.

Maybe you've believed in God most of your life. Perhaps you've even viewed Him as a God of love. Yet when you look at the Bible, things get complicated. It seems conflicting, especially when you read about such things as hell and eternal punishment. These don't appear to line up with God's mercy and kindness toward people. Perhaps this has raised some questions in your mind.

"What is God really like? Will He punish me when I die, or will He love and accept me? Does He personally care about me? How can I know for sure? What about my life here and now? Is there a purpose for me other than what I see? If so, what is it?"

You might be surprised to learn that God isn't as mysterious as we think. He has always wanted us to know the answers to these questions, and more. There is one in particular that I believe He wants us to intimately know the answer to..."who is God?"

This book is my discovery of who God is.

What is presented within will help remove a veil of mystery that seems to surround God and His intent for mankind. With the veil removed, you will be able to see what He has always wanted you to see...the reason you exist.

Will everyone eventually get to be with God forever?

Does His love finally win in the end?

Come along with me on a journey of discovery my friend. You are about to find out.

1

From the Beginning

As far back as I can remember I understood that life wouldn't last forever. Even as a young boy, when life was just beginning to unfold, I realized that everything I would experience on earth would someday come to an end. Nobody had to tell me this. I just knew.

I didn't think about it much though while growing up in Seattle Washington during the 1960's. I was too busy playing "army" and building forts in the woods with my childhood friends. There was a world that needed to be explored and enemies to be conquered. We'd spend all summer long from morning to evening engaged in combat, rescuing people, and killing the bad guys.

Then along came The Beatles. We switched from building forts to making pretend guitars out of plywood. Instead of playing army with each other, we played concerts for our parents, complete with music from our record player. We charged twenty-five cents for admission and made enough money to ride our bikes down to the local ice-creamery to celebrate our successful gig.

When the 70's hit, it was high school track and running clubs. We competed in events all around our city. We ran with some well-known runners at the time...even "streaked" with them. Yeah, it was the 70's. We were jocks, daring, and reckless.

My senior year of high school was a turning point in life. Following in the footsteps of my father and uncles, I joined the U.S. Navy. None of my friends signed up with me so we said our goodbyes after graduating and I set off to sail the seas. I was on my way to a life of adventure for however long it would last.

Throughout my time of military service I never did get stationed on a ship. Instead, I ended up being landlocked on an island in the west Pacific Ocean...not quite the adventure I envisioned. Decades earlier, Okinawa was the scene of some of the bloodiest battles of World War 2. When I arrived, it looked nothing like a strategic military objective worth fighting for. Still it was there that I experienced the greatest event of my life. It far surpassed any adventure that I could have ever imagined.

A few months after I arrived on the island, the unit I was assigned to received a new supervisor. He was Gunnery Sergeant Chuck Truitt who had made the U.S. Marine Corps his lifelong career. As a Navy man I tried to avoid him like the plague. He was a "lifer" and too military for me. There was something else about him too. He carried a Bible with him tucked under his arm. I thought, "Great, a Bible thumper. He's going to hammer us with religion when he gets the chance." So whenever I saw him, I pretended to be busy or on my way to someplace else.

This worked out really well...until one day.

I had just finished an evening shift and had started down a hallway to leave the operations building where I worked when I heard someone behind me call out. "Hey, Seaman! Can I talk with you for a moment?"

Uh-oh. I recognized that voice. It was Gunny Truitt, the lifer. I quickly tried to think of an excuse for not being able to talk, but couldn't come up with one. So I reluctantly agreed, telling him that I only had a moment to give.

That was all he needed.

Truitt asked if he could show me something in the Bible that I would find really important, even life changing. Before I could tell him no thanks, I said "yeah, sure", surprising myself that I had said yes.

Truitt pulled his Bible from under his arm and opened it. He pointed out passages of scripture and read them out loud. He had me read along with him. There was something in his voice as he read...something that I hadn't experienced before. It was compassion. He had a genuine concern for me as he spoke. He showed me that God, the Creator of the universe, loved me and wanted to have a relationship with me. But my sin was keeping this from happening. It was taking me down the path to certain eternal death. So He sent Jesus, His Son, to die on the cross and pay the penalty that I deserved for my sin. He died for me! Through Him I can be forgiven and enter into this relationship and be saved from where I was ultimately headed.

It was the first time I had heard anything like this. I grew up in a religious environment and went to a church almost every Sunday for years. But I had never heard this taught. It wasn't even mentioned.

It's hard to describe all that happened in those few minutes. It was a life or death moment for me. The words Truitt spoke and the words I read in the Bible got my full attention. I was loved by God! He wanted to forgive me, save me, and give me life with Him forever. At the same time, I didn't want to go to hell. The thought of ending up there shook me. It was then that I realized the life I was living wasn't taking me where I thought I was going.

I was convicted. I believed what Gunny Truitt said was true. Up till then most everything I had done and chased after was to please myself. I was the "god" of my life. Still there was no real sense of fulfillment in any of it. When I was shown God's personal love for me, I saw then what my life really consisted of, and it wasn't what He wanted for me. It was my selfish sin. I asked Jesus to forgive me, save me, and be the Lord of my life. I was later baptized in His name as I openly confessed my faith in Him.

Something dramatic happened to me that day I was baptized. I find it almost impossible to describe.

After being baptized, I went into a changing room to dry off and get dressed. I had just gotten my clothes on and was about to walk out of the room when it happened. I felt something like a dark heaviness being lifted off of me. I could actually feel it leaving. It was the most freeing sensation I have ever experienced. As it lifted, a profound joy entered deep inside me. God's life and love literally came into my soul. I felt really alive for the first time in my life. At that moment I knew that I was personally forgiven, and loved, and saved by God. I weep as I share this with you. It was an intimate encounter with Him that goes beyond words.

Since that day, I've been living a true life adventure. It has taken me from the west Pacific Ocean to the Middle East and Europe, enabling me to share with others what God has given me. And honestly, I can't think of a better way to spend the few short years I have here on earth than doing just this.

Through all that I've experienced, I've come to realize it was never God's desire for anyone to be eternally separated from Him. From the beginning, He created mankind to have life with Him and spend all eternity exploring His creation and experiencing the depth of His love. It's immeasurable. But because of sin, we lost what we were created for. What Adam did in the Garden of Eden long ago brought a judgment of eternal death upon everyone. But this hasn't stopped God from fulfilling His desire. His love for us is so enduring that He's provided a way to bring us back to life with Him.

There is a teaching that is gaining popularity today which claims to explain what God has done to bring mankind back to Himself. It has impacted the lives of many people. It challenges what is generally understood about the gospel of Jesus and provides a very different explanation of the salvation that God offers to mankind. It's called "Christian Universalism", or more commonly referred to as "Universalism".

There are many resources available in print and on the internet that explain Universalism in detail. I don't attempt to do that here. Instead, I summarize what this doctrine proposes by addressing the main concepts it contains.

In a nutshell, the doctrine of Universalism declares that all of mankind will ultimately be saved from the consequence of sin. Jesus Christ's death on the cross, as atonement for man's sin, is universal and applies to all. Therefore every person who has ever existed will eventually be reconciled to God and will live with Him forever.

Within Universalism is the premise that every human being is a child of God created in His image. Therefore, God is the Father of every person. And as Father, the eternal punishment for sin that occurs after a person has died without faith in Christ comes from a father's love for his children and is corrective in purpose not condemning. Also, God is love (1 John 4:8). Because *"love never fails"* (1 Corinthians 13:8) and *"mercy triumphs over judgment"* (James 2:13), eternal punishment for sin is temporary and ultimately purges people of their wrong doing. After having been cleansed, they will then become acceptable to God, released from the eternal judgment, and mercifully allowed entrance into His heavenly kingdom.

Universalism proposes that a just and loving God would never punish any person forever because of sin. It's not in His nature to do so. God is loving and merciful. He will eventually reconcile all things to Himself (Colossians 1:20), even people who enter the eternal judgment. All things will be summed up in Christ (Ephesians 1:10), and all things will be subjected to Him (1 Corinthians 15:28). When they are, God will then be *"all in all"* (1 Corinthians 15:28) with all of mankind having eternal life with Him.

Many who once believed that faith in Christ during this lifetime is exclusively how a person is saved from the eternal consequence for sin now admit that they no longer believe this. Universalism has fundamentally changed what they believe about God and the salvation that He provides. They've come to sincerely think that every human being who has ever existed will eventually get to spend eternity with God in His kingdom.

Sincerity is important. But does being sincere guarantee that what we think about something is correct?

In the New Testament book of Acts (chapters 10 & 11), an account is given of a genuinely sincere and God-fearing man named Cornelius. This man was generous, devout, and prayed to God continually. Through a vision, God sent Cornelius an angel instructing him to *"Send men to Joppa, and call for Simon whose surname is Peter, who will tell you words by which you and all your household will be saved"* (Acts 11:14 NKJV). If Cornelius would have eventually received salvation after he died, as Universalism proposes, why did God send an angel to tell him that he must find Peter and listen to a message that *"will"* save him?

Though he was sincere, Cornelius would have perished had Peter not been sent to him. What he was trusting in could not save him. Cornelius needed to hear the truth about Jesus. When he heard from Peter that *"everyone who believes in Him receives forgiveness of sins"*, he and his entire household believed. The moment they did, the Holy Spirit came upon them and on that day they were saved.

I can identify with Cornelius. The things we both sincerely thought regarding life fell eternally short. We needed to be rescued. Someone needed to come and tell us the truth so that we could be saved from eternal destruction.

If being sincere is no guarantee, how can we know for certain that what we understand about God and the salvation He provides is really true?

The way to know is to compare what we understand with what God says. He has given us a written testament, the Bible, so that we can clearly know what He has done for us.

My intent in examining Universalism isn't to question the sincerity of those embracing it. It's to look at the foundation on which it's built. Universalism is built upon a number of assertions. One that it relies heavily upon is "God is the Father of every person". I start by looking at what scripture says about the Fatherhood of God and go on from there. It's easy to get overly detailed and obscure the simplicity of truth so I tried to write in a way that's easy to understand, letting scripture interpret scripture.

I hope that what I have written will help you to see, and clearly understand, God's offer of salvation to mankind. I also hope that God personally reveals Himself to you and that you come to intimately experience the love He has for you.

Allow yourself time to read all of the scriptures that are referenced, even though you might already be familiar with them. Examine what I write in light of God's word. If necessary, read again any portion that you have difficulty understanding. Ask God to remove any confusion that you might encounter and to guide you into the truth.

He will!

2

Questions Worth Asking

I once attended a gathering of friends who were looking into the prospect of universal salvation. For some time they had been listening to various teachers and reading articles claiming that all of mankind would eventually be reconciled to God. They decided to get together to talk about this in depth. As I listened to what they discussed I was a little shocked. The comments they made stood in challenge to what I understood about God and how He saves people. I sat quietly taking note of the things that were spoken.

There was a lot of speculating about the meaning of certain words and scriptures. This led to some strange conclusions about what the Bible teaches. In the end, things were said and proposed which contradicted the clear and simple message of the gospel. I left the gathering heavy hearted. These were people I knew and loved, and still do. My wife and I spent years with many of them enjoying our friendships while serving God and each other. What I witnessed made me deeply concerned. The idea of universal salvation had led my friends to conclude things about God and salvation that I understood weren't true.

After that meeting I spent days praying and reading the Bible. Could the things that my friends proposed really be true? Will God eventually save everyone? Was I wrong in what I had believed for so long? I really wanted to know.

In time, God gave me understanding and peace. He also encouraged me to respond to my friends and entreat them to reconsider what they were concluding about universal salvation. I carefully wrote out my response and sent it to them via an email.

Within a couple of days I received replies.

Many had criticized what I had written. One person in particular said that what I communicated wasn't very "scholarly". I admit that I didn't like this comment at first. I worked hard to be thorough yet considerate and entreating. But then I realized something. This might actually be a compliment. I remembered that it was the scholars of Jesus' day who missed what He said about salvation. This helped me to be grateful that I didn't take a scholarly approach to convey what God had given me to say.

I'm not a theologian. I'm just an average guy wanting to know the truth. I have questions just like anyone else. That day with my friends helped to bring a few of these out in the open.

I hope the questions asked here help you to know what is true about God and how he saves people. Perhaps they are ones that you also have been wanting answers to.

Is God the Father of every person?

Not everyone who says to Me, 'Lord, Lord,' will enter the kingdom of heaven, but he who does the will of my Father in heaven will enter (Matthew 7:21 NASB).

...Nor are they all children because they are the seed of Abraham...those who are the children of the flesh, these are not the children of God; but the children of the promise are counted as the seed (Romans 9:7-8 NKJV).

No one who is born of God practices sin, because His seed abides in him, and he cannot sin, because he is born of God. By this the children of God and the children of the devil are obvious (1 John 3:9-10 NASB).

I am the way, and the truth, and the life; no one comes to the Father but through Me (John 14:6 NASB).

Whoever denies the Son does not have the Father; the one who confesses the Son has the Father also (1 John 2:23 NASB).

...Nor does anyone know the Father except the Son, and anyone to whom the Son wills to reveal Him (Matthew 11:27 NASB).

There is a consistent theme portrayed throughout the New Testament of the Bible. God is a Father. We know this because of Jesus, His Son.

During the three and a half years He ministered here on earth, Jesus often spoke of God as "Father". He told His disciples that the words He spoke and the works He performed were literally from the Father. He used an encounter that He had with certain Jewish leaders of His day to reveal the truth about God's Fatherhood to those who followed Him (John 8:12-59).

As Jesus taught in the temple, many were coming to believe in Him. The leading Pharisees saw this as a threat to their place of prominence among the people so they tried to find fault with His testimony in order to discredit Him. They challenged what Jesus said about the Father and the relationship that He has with Him. Jesus knew what they were trying to do and used it as an opportunity to teach those around Him who God is the Father of.

You know neither Me nor My Father; if you knew Me, you would know My Father also (John 8:19 NASB).

Jesus revealed three things in this one statement. First, these Pharisees did not know Jesus or His Father. The word "know" used here means "to know in fullness". Second, God is *His* Father. He was intentionally exclusive in referring to the Fatherhood of God. Third, the way to know His Father is through knowing Him.

Jesus is the only one who knows the Father and reveals Him exclusively to those whom He chooses. He said, *"...nor does anyone know the Father except the Son, and anyone to whom the Son wills to reveal Him"* (Matthew 11:27 NASB). No one can know God as Father any other way.

Jesus went on to explain more to those gathered around Him.

If you continue in My word, then you are truly disciples of Mine; and you will know the truth, and the truth will make you free (John 8:31-32 NASB).

The Pharisees took exception to these words. They proclaimed they were the descendants of the great Jewish patriarch Abraham and had never been enslaved to anyone. So how could Jesus say they would be *"free"* if they weren't slaves? Jesus told them.

Truly, truly, I say to you, everyone who commits sin is the slave of sin. The slave does not remain in the house forever; the son does remain forever. So if the Son makes you free, you will be free indeed. I know that you are Abraham's descendants; yet you seek to kill Me, because My word has no place in you. I speak the things which I have seen with My

Father; therefore you also do the things which you heard from your father (John 8:34-38 NASB).

Jesus confronted these Pharisees. Though they were Abraham's descendants, they were not doing what Abraham did. In fact, they sought to kill Jesus. *"If you are Abraham's children, do the deeds of Abraham. But as it is, you are seeking to kill Me, a man who has told you the truth, which I heard from God; this Abraham did not do. You are doing the deeds of your father"* (John 8:40-41 NASB). The things they were doing exposed their true spiritual condition. They were not free as they claimed. They were slaves of sin. This proved their spiritual lineage was from someone other than Abraham.

What did Abraham do that these people were not doing?

Long ago, God spoke to Abraham about His intent to bless him and make him a great nation. Though he couldn't physically see Him, Abraham believed God. Because he did, his faith was credited to him as righteousness. He received right standing with God and eternal life with Him through responding to what God said with faith. Abraham was the forerunner of all who would be freed from sin through faith. He is the father of those who believe (Romans 4:11). And now God in the flesh (John 1:1-14) was speaking with these people, face to face, but they would not believe. They refused to receive what Jesus said. They were not like Abraham at all.

Having lost the argument regarding Abraham, they then tried to justify themselves another way. *"We were not born of fornication; we have one Father: God"* (John 8:41 NASB). They claimed their lineage was pure because God himself was their Father!

Then Jesus got to the heart of the matter and identified who their real father was.

> *If God were your Father, you would love Me, for I proceeded forth and have come from God, for I have not even come on My own initiative, but He sent Me. Why do you not understand what I am saying? It is because you cannot hear My word. You are of your father the devil, and you want to do the desires of your father. He was a murderer from the beginning, and does not stand in the truth because there is no truth in him. Whenever he speaks a lie, he speaks from his own nature, for he is a liar and the father of lies. But because I speak the truth, you do not believe Me. Which one of you convicts Me of sin? If I speak truth, why do you not believe Me? He who is of God hears the words of God; for this reason you do not hear them, because you are not of God* (John 8:42-47 NASB).

Jesus told them straight out. God was not their Father. Their father was Satan.

These Jews tried to claim God as their Father but couldn't. They did not believe or know Jesus. Knowing Jesus is prerequisite for anyone to be able to rightfully claim God as their Father. They opposed Him as He spoke the truth. This revealed their true condition. They were *"not of God"* and would not receive His word, just as Jesus said. Their unbelief kept them in slavery to sin.

Throughout history there have been people who have thought that simply being human makes someone a child of God. Since God created man in His image, and He is a heavenly Father as scripture says, then mankind must be His children. God is therefore the Father of everyone.

God did create Adam with His image. But because of sin, Adam lost what God gave him and took on a different nature. His nature became that of Satan, the one who *"sinned from the beginning"* (1 John 3:8 NKJV), the one Adam relinquished himself to by choice. As a result, Adam became a dead man, dead in sin. Since then, mankind has been guilty of sin, spiritually dead, and experiencing the consequence of having the sinful nature of Satan.

Through this encounter Jesus showed us that there are people who do not belong to God. Sadly, they reject Jesus when He comes to them. To these He said, *"...because I speak the truth, you do not believe me"* (John 8:45 NASB). They did not believe Him because they would not receive the love of the truth and be saved (2 Thessalonians 2:10). As with Satan, they reject the truth to their own demise. This is why in scripture they are referred to as *"children of wrath"* (Ephesians 2:1-3) and *"sons of disobedience"* (Ephesians 5:5-6).

Coming into the world through natural birth does not make someone a child of God, nor does being a descendant of Abraham (Romans 9:7-8). God is the Father of those who become His offspring through the work of His Holy Spirit (John 3:6). He, the Spirit, is God's promise to man for kinship. The indwelling of His Spirit through spiritual rebirth makes us His child, not the natural procreation of man.

For anyone to be able to call God their Father, they must first be "related" to Him. Just as no one can rightfully say that someone is their father here on earth unless they are related to that person, so it is with God. Knowing Jesus, and being in a relationship of love with Him through the Holy Spirit, enables us to call God our Father. Adherence to Mosaic Law, or any other claim of association with Him, cannot produce this relational connection. Only love can. *"If God were your Father, you would love Me,"* Jesus said (John 8:42 NASB). God is the Father of those who love Jesus.

> *For the Father Himself loves you, because you have loved Me and have believed that I came forth from the Father* (John 16:27 NASB).

God is the creator of all but clearly not the Father of all. The privilege to call Him "Father" is reserved for those who believe and love His Son. These are the ones which the Father has relationship with. These are His Spiritual children who are being transformed into the likeness of Jesus.

An eternal destiny to know God as Father hinges on what we do when He personally reveals our sin to us. Will we acknowledge the truth, repent, and ask for His forgiveness? Or will we resist Him? Jesus openly showed God's love for us by dying in our place to take away sin. Will we respond to Him with love in return by openly receiving what He has done for us?

God will never force anyone to love Him. He lets us choose whether or not we will love Him in return.

To those who do, Jesus says, *"...I ascend to My Father and your Father, and My God and your God"* (John 20:17 NASB).

How does someone become a child of God?

> *But as many as received Him, to them He gave the right to become children of God, to those who believe in His name: who were born, not of blood, nor of the will of the flesh, nor of the will of man, but of God* (John 1:12-13 NASB).

> *For as many as are led by the Spirit of God, these are sons of God. For you did not receive the spirit*

of bondage again to fear, but you received the Spirit of adoption by whom we cry out, 'Abba, Father.' The Spirit Himself bears witness with our spirit that we are children of God, and if children, then heirs—heirs of God and joint heirs with Christ... (Romans 8:14-17 NKJV).

For you are all sons of God through faith in Christ Jesus (Galatians 3:26 NKJV).

He saved us, not on the basis of deeds which we have done in righteousness, but according to His mercy, by the washing of regeneration and renewing by the Holy Spirit... (Titus 3:5 NASB).

Truly, truly, I say to you, unless one is born again he cannot see the kingdom of God...unless one is born of water and the Spirit he cannot enter the kingdom of God (John 3:3-5 NASB).

Offspring are produced by way of relationship, whether naturally or spiritually. To become a child of God and possess eternal life, we must enter into a relationship with Him through His eternal Son. Jesus is the way, the truth and the life. No one can come to the Father apart from Him (John 14:6).

The way we become His child is by receiving Jesus in faith (Galatians 3:26). God doesn't force us to receive His Son against our will nor does He force us to love Him. If He did He wouldn't be love. But because He is love (1 John 4:8), He allows us to choose whether or not to love Him. As Jesus said, those who belong to God will receive and love Him (John 8:42). When we receive Jesus, the Holy Spirit comes to dwell in us. It is the work of the Holy Spirit that makes us a new creation in Christ and a child of God.

When we repent of our sin and trust Jesus for salvation, God forgives us and cleanses us of our sin. He seals us in Him with His Holy Spirit. Through *"the spirit of adoption"* (Romans 8:15) we receive His Spirit as a pledge of our inheritance...redemption! The miraculous work of the Holy Spirit makes us a new creation by transforming our nature, our very being. He removes our sin and gives us God's sinless nature. He regenerates us (Titus 3:5) into being a child of God!

This work of the Spirit is taking place here on earth during this present age. We are born once of the flesh to enter this world. We need to be born a second time, of the Spirit, in order to enter the kingdom of heaven. This is why Jesus told Nicodemus, a ruler of the Jews, *"You must be born again"* (John 3:7 NASB).

Spiritual rebirth is the only way into God's kingdom (John 3:5). It's also the only way anyone can become a child of God.

Is the punishment of unbelievers the same as the chastening God gives His children?

But when we are judged, we are disciplined by the Lord so that we will not be condemned along with the world (1 Corinthians 11:32 NASB).

...My son, do not despise the chastening of the Lord, nor be discouraged when you are rebuked by him; For whom the Lord loves He chastens, and scourges every son whom He receives...for what son is there whom his father does not discipline? (Hebrews 12:5-7 NKJV).

It is actually reported that there is immorality among you, and immorality of such a kind as does not exist even among the Gentiles, that someone has his father's wife...deliver such a one to Satan for the destruction of the flesh, that his spirit may be saved in the day of the Lord Jesus (1 Corinthians 5:1-5 NKJV).

...When the Lord Jesus will be revealed from heaven with His mighty angels in flaming fire, dealing out retribution to those who do not know God and to those who do not obey the gospel of our Lord Jesus. These will pay the penalty of eternal destruction, away from the presence of the Lord and from the glory of His power, when He comes to be glorified in His saints on that day, and to be marveled at among all who have believed--for our testimony to you was believed (2 Thessalonians 1:6-10 NASB).

For many walk, of whom I have told you often, and now tell you even weeping, that they are the enemies of the cross of Christ: whose end is destruction... (Philippians 3:18-19 NKJV).

The doctrine of Universalism confuses the punishment of unbelievers with God's disciplining of His children. The two are not the same. This confusion is the result of not understanding the Fatherhood of God. Once we know the truth of His Fatherhood, we can then see there is a vast difference between the two.

The chastening of those who belong to God occurs here on earth. This is done by the Holy Spirit who comes to dwell in believers. The work of the Spirit to discipline us through life circumstances causes us to become more like Jesus. Everyone who is in Christ can testify to this. We've all gone through times of painful correction as our sinful tendencies have been dealt with. We experience the careful pruning of the "Vinedresser" so that we grow in Christ and bear the fruit of His Spirit. The tribulations we endure here are designed to produce Godly character in us (Romans 5:3-5). This is God's way of disciplining His children so that we can share in His holiness. We might not enjoy it at times, but after we've been trained by it, there comes *"the peaceful fruit of righteousness"* (Hebrews 12:7-11 NASB).

This corrective discipline is what distinguishes us as God's children.

In his letter to the church in Corinth, Paul rebukes the Corinthian believers of his day who were tolerating sexual immorality among themselves. One of them had fallen so far as to have sexual relations with his father's wife! Paul told them to deliver that man over to Satan for the destruction of his flesh so that his spirit may be saved in the day of the Lord Jesus. We don't know exactly what the destruction of his flesh entailed. But it is clear it would prevent him from continuing on in sin. This may be the severest form of correction that a believer can experience here on earth. Paul then reminded them that though he has nothing to do with judging outsiders (unbelievers), there is supposed to be a Godly judging of those who are within the church (1 Corinthians 5:12).

Paul loved the believers at Corinth. He worked hard to help them grow in Christ. At times he was blunt when a situation required him to be. This was one of those times.

Admittedly it seems harsh but there was a loving purpose behind the chastening of this believer. This taking place in his lifetime would result in a favorable eternal outcome later on. If it didn't happen, this man would fall to judgment and not be saved. Paul wanted believers to understand the serious consequence of willful participation in sin.

God loves His children immensely. He is deeply concerned when they become ensnared in destructive behavior. His chastening of us in love is truly redeeming.

There is a distinct difference between the chastening of believers and the punishment of unbelievers.

God lovingly brings correction to believers during their life on earth. It is meant to transform their character and produce the life of Christ in them. The punishment of unbelievers happens after they die. It involves "the second death" in the lake of fire (Revelation 20:14-15). It is meant for the destruction of their soul.

The punishment of unbelievers in the lake of fire is eternally devastating. It is neither redemptive nor corrective as Universalism proposes. It is punitive and destructive. Its purpose is the eternal destruction of man (Matthew 10:28). It cannot remove sin, produce the fruit of the Spirit, or make anyone like Jesus. It's the place of God's eternal wrath against man for sin (Romans 2:5). Death in the lake of fire cannot produce eternal life. Eternal life is only produced by the Spirit of life which is in Jesus alone (Romans 8:2).

We must understand that those who are cast into the lake of fire at the judgment will not be redeemed. They will not be redeemed because man cannot pay the price of his redemption in any way...even by suffering eternal torment. Redemption can only be found in the Redeemer, the Savior Jesus, who saves from the wrath to come (1 Thessalonians 1:10). He has already paid the price in full with HIS suffering (Ephesians 1:7; 1 Peter 2:21)!

God truly loves us and does not want anyone to perish in the lake of fire. This is why He is calling out for us to come to Him NOW to be saved.

How are people saved?

...Jesus came into Galilee, preaching the gospel of God, and saying, 'The time is fulfilled, and the kingdom of God is at hand; repent and believe in the gospel' (Mark 1:15 NASB).

Go into all the world and preach the gospel to all creation. He who has believed and has been baptized shall be saved; but he who has disbelieved shall be condemned (Mark 16:15-16 NASB).

...That whoever believes in Him shall not perish, but have eternal life (John 3:16 NASB).

...'Sirs, what must I do to be saved?' So they said, 'Believe on the Lord Jesus Christ, and you will be saved, you and your household.' Then they spoke the word of the Lord to him and to all who were in his house (Acts 16:29-32 NKJV).

...If you confess with your mouth Jesus as Lord and believe in your heart that God raised Him from the dead, you will be saved; for with the heart a person believes, resulting in righteousness and with the mouth he confesses, resulting in salvation...for whoever will call upon the name of the Lord will be saved (Romans 10:9-13 NASB).

...It pleased God through the foolishness of the message preached to save those who believe (1 Corinthians 1:21 NKJV).

'Zacchaeus, hurry and come down, for today I must stay at your house.' And he hurried and came down and received Him gladly...'Today salvation has come to this house... for the Son of Man has come to seek and to save that which was lost' (Luke 19:5-10 NASB).

The story of Zacchaeus in the Gospel of Luke is a beautiful illustration of salvation.

Zacchaeus was a despised tax collector who made himself rich with other people's money. He heard that Jesus was passing through his area. But because of the crowd of people surrounding Jesus, Zacchaeus had to climb up into to a tree in order to see Him.

When Jesus came to that place, He looked up and said, *"Zacchaeus, hurry and come down, for today I must stay at your house."* What happened next changed Zacchaeus' life forever. Zacchaeus hurried down and *"received Him gladly."* He then stopped and said to Jesus, *"Behold, Lord, half of my possessions I will give to the poor, and if I have defrauded anyone of anything, I will give back four times as much"* (Luke 19:8 NASB).

Jesus tells us what happened. *"Today salvation has come to this house"*. Zacchaeus was saved that day because he *received* Jesus! The moment he did his heart was miraculously changed.

Salvation isn't shrouded in mystery. It's transparent for all who, by faith, receive.

Satan is a cunning adversary. He entices people with speculation to rob them of the obvious. So that we don't fall prey to his tactic, let's look at the obvious.

What do all of the above mentioned scriptures regarding salvation have in common?

The opportunity to receive Jesus by faith and be saved is given to those who are alive on earth. This opportunity is not given to those who have died.

Wouldn't God explicitly tell us how we could be saved after we die if it were possible? But He doesn't. Why?

It's because He IS telling us how to be saved. The way to be saved is through faith in His crucified Son while we are alive on earth so that we won't die in our sins and perish.

Salvation comes by way of relationship with Jesus. Knowing Him is eternal life (John 17:3). "For all of you who were baptized into Christ have clothed yourselves with Christ" (Galatians 3:27 NASB). God gives us the opportunity to "clothe ourselves with Christ" and enter into a relationship with Him here on earth before we expire. We no longer have this opportunity after we die.

> ...It is appointed for men to die once and after this comes judgment (Hebrews 9:27 NASB).

I thank God for the simplicity of the gospel. It reveals the genuine compassion He has for us. He wants us to understand how we can be saved. We don't have to jump through theological hoops to know. In receiving Jesus, we receive eternal life and are saved.

What about those who haven't heard the Gospel?

> All that the Father gives Me will come to me, and the one who comes to Me I will certainly not cast out (John 6:37 NASB).

> Jesus answered and said to them, 'Do not grumble among yourselves. No one can come to Me unless the Father who sent Me draws him; and I will raise him up on the last day' (John 6:43-44).

> ...Everyone who has heard and learned from the Father, comes to Me (John 6:45).

> Of those whom You have given Me I lost not one (John 18:9 NASB).

> However, they did not all heed the good news; for Isaiah says, 'Lord, who has believed our report?' So

faith comes from hearing, and hearing by the word of Christ. But I say, surely they have never heard, have they? Indeed they have; 'Their voice has gone out into all the earth, and their words to the ends of the world' (Romans 10:17-18 NASB).

But we should always give thanks to God for you, brethren beloved by the Lord, because God has chosen you from the beginning for salvation through sanctification by the Spirit and faith in the truth (2 Thessalonians 2:13 NASB).

For many are called, but few are chosen (Matthew 22:14 NKJV).

What about those who haven't heard the gospel? Will they be eternally lost because they didn't hear about Jesus and believe in Him before they died...even if they were devout and God-fearing?

I believe the short answer to this question, sadly, is yes. People who have not heard about Jesus before they die will not be saved.

In the Old Testament era, salvation was given to those who believed God and responded to Him in faith when He personally revealed Himself to them. God credited this faith as righteousness (Romans 4:3). In the New Testament era, salvation is given to those who repent and believe in the person of Jesus because God is now revealing Himself through Him (Hebrews 1:2). To be saved today, a person must have faith in Jesus for righteousness to be credited to him (Romans 4:5; Philippians 3:9). To believe in Jesus, a person must hear about Him. (Remember the story of Cornelius in the book of Acts.) How can anyone believe in Him whom they have not heard (Romans 10:14)? The answer is evident. They can't. This is why the gospel must be preached. In hearing the good news about Jesus, people are given the opportunity to believe and be saved (Romans 10:8-17).

> *For since in the wisdom of God the world through its wisdom did not come to know God, God was well-pleased through the foolishness of the message preached to save those who believe* (1 Corinthians 1:21).

God saves people through the foolishness of preaching the gospel of Jesus. Those "foolish" enough to believe the message they hear are granted salvation. God's wisdom to save people this way confounds our human wisdom and understanding.

Isn't it unjust for someone to be eternally condemned for not hearing about Jesus? It's not their fault that they didn't hear, is it?

It would be unjust for someone who is innocent to be eternally condemned. But are those who haven't heard about Jesus innocent?

People aren't at fault for not hearing about Jesus. They're at fault for being guilty of something that consigns them to eternal judgment.

> *For God did not send the Son into the world to judge the world, but that the world might be saved through Him. He who believes in Him is not judged; he who does not believe has been judged already, because he has not believed in the name of the only begotten Son of God* (John 3:17-18 NASB).

According to Jesus, people are at fault because of unbelief. The apostle John confirms this in Revelation 21:8. Not believing in Jesus will ultimately consign a person to the eternal judgment.

Notice that Jesus spoke about being judged in the past tense, *"...has been judged already"*. He is telling us that mankind has already been judged. Mankind having been judged is the reason that God sent His Son into the world to offer the way of escape.

Long ago, because of disobedience to God by the first man Adam, mankind was judged. Adam brought this upon himself through his sinful wrong doing. Since we are his offspring, we possess his same sinful nature. He made us to be sinners when he sinned (Romans 5:19). As such, we are under the same judgment that Adam placed himself under.

Before He went to the cross, Jesus told His disciples that He was going to send the Spirit of truth to convict the world of sin (John 16:8-13). The Spirit of truth convicts the world of sin because the world does not believe in Jesus.

And He, when He comes, will convict the world concerning sin and righteousness and judgment; concerning sin, because they do not believe in Me (John 16:8-9 NASB).

We all enter this world not believing in Jesus and subject to sin. Because of this we are guilty. This is why it is so critical that the good news of Jesus be preached. God forgives us when we are no longer unbelieving. When we personally repent and believe in Jesus, He removes our sin and guilt from us. Through faith in Him we are saved from the eternal judgement of death that Adam brought upon us and are given the eternal life that Jesus has with the Father.

People's salvation depends upon their hearing this good news. Dying in unbelief with their sin unforgiven will separate one from God forever (John 8:21-24).

Does this mean that people from remote areas of the world or places apparently closed to the gospel won't hear about Jesus?

Possibly so.

There is no way we can know with certainty that someone has not heard about Jesus unless we ask them personally. Until we do this, we can only assume they haven't. Even though they might not have heard, this does not stop God from fulfilling His plan to bring people to Himself.

Jesus said, *"All that the Father gives me will come to me, and the one who comes to Me I will certainly not cast out"* (John 6:37 NASB). All those the Father gives to Jesus *will* come to Him, no matter where on earth they happen to be. This means that each one who is given to Him hears about Him. Hearing about Jesus is the only way that anyone can come to believe in Him and be saved. Jesus also said that no person can come to Him unless God the Father draws him (John 6:44).

Through Jesus we learn that God the Father is the initiator of salvation. He makes sure that every person He gives to His Son hears about forgiveness and salvation being offered through Him. But hearing alone does not save anyone. Those who respond in faith when they hear are the ones who are saved.

God's offer of salvation is to all mankind. He doesn't want anyone to perish. *"The Lord is not slow about His promise, as some count slowness, but is patient toward you, not wishing for any to perish but for all to come to repentance"* (2 Peter 3:9 NASB). He has extended an invitation to everyone. *"Whoever will call upon the name of the Lord will be saved"* (Romans 10:13 NASB). *"Whoever believes in Him will have eternal life"* (John 3:15 NASB). "Whoever believes" means "all who believe" or "anyone who believes".

How can eternal life be given to "anyone" when only those who are drawn by the Father come to Jesus? Isn't this a contradiction?

No, there is no contradiction. God does give eternal life to anyone who believes in His Son. For anyone to believe in Him, they must first be drawn to Him by the Father. It is the Father who connects people to the Son.

Does this mean that God chooses those who will be saved?

Yes! Well, more accurately, He already has chosen. God did His choosing a long time ago.

But we should always give thanks to God for you, brethren beloved by the Lord, because God has chosen you from the beginning for salvation through sanctification by the Spirit and faith in the truth. It was for this He called you through our gospel, that you may gain the glory of our Lord Jesus Christ (2 Thessalonians 2:13 NASB).

...Just as He chose us in Him before the foundation of the world, that we would be holy and blameless before Him. In love He predestined us to adoption as sons through Jesus Christ to Himself, according to the kind intention of His will (Ephesians 1:4-5 NASB).

Long ago, God chose to give eternal life to those who would believe Him at His word. People who would respond by faith, taking to heart and acting upon the word He speaks to them, would enjoy life with Him forever. In the beginning, God gave His word to the first man Adam. Had Adam kept His word and not eaten from the forbidden tree, he would have been able to eat from the other tree that was in the Garden of Eden...the tree of life. If he had eaten from this tree, he would have lived forever (Genesis 3:22). But Adam didn't keep God's word. As a result, man lost the opportunity to have the life God wanted Him to have.

Today, God is speaking to us through His Son (Hebrews 1:1-2). His words are from the Father (John 12:49-50). His words are eternal life (John 6:63). If we do not receive what He says, we will not receive eternal life.

Jesus said, *"Everyone who has heard and learned from the Father, comes to me"* (John 6:45 NASB). This reveals a mystery that we don't fully understand. The Father works in people's lives before they come to believe in His Son. By His Spirit, He brings them to the moment when they hear the truth about Jesus. When they hear, they are given an opportunity to believe what they hear. Those who have learned from the Father believe in Jesus. Those who have not learned from Him do not believe.

Learning *"from the Father"* is essential for a person to come to faith in Christ. Learning from the Father simply means to receive what He speaks and reveals about what is true. This happens in a mysterious way. Most of the time, we don't realize that God does this until after we come to faith in Jesus. In the course of our life, He reveals things to us. Though He reveals things, He doesn't force us to accept or believe what He reveals. He leaves that to us. If we do receive what He reveals, we learn from Him. How much we learn depends upon how willing we are to receive. Learning from the Father in this way enables us to receive further revelation when He brings it.

God can tell us life changing truths and show us astounding miracles. But if we don't receive what He reveals, we do not learn from Him. This is why Jesus said that everyone who has heard *and learned* from the Father comes to Him. Those who had learned from what the Father revealed to them up to that point were drawn to Jesus when He was presented. Those who didn't learn from the Father were not drawn to Him. They did not believe and would not receive the love of the truth to be saved (2 Thessalonians 2:10).

Does God reveal truth to everyone or just a select few?

Since God does not want anyone to perish, wouldn't it be in keeping with this desire to reveal truth in some way to everyone? I believe He does. What we do with what He reveals is up to us.

God invites all to have a relationship with Him and enjoy the abundant eternal blessings therein. Though He invites all, not everyone accepts His invitation. There were many people in Jesus' day who heard about Him. They heard the words He spoke and even witnessed the miracles He performed. Everything Jesus did was according to the will of the Father to reveal His love for people and His desire for all to come to Him. They heard and saw but would not believe. Sadly, their unbelief prevented them from receiving the life God freely offered them.

The call to receive eternal life has gone out. It's spreading throughout the whole earth. Many are hearing about what God is offering through His Son. Those responding to the call with faith are repenting and accepting His invitation to life.

The Father knows every single person He is giving to His Son. Though the Father knows who they are, we do not! This is why Jesus told His disciples to go into all the world and preach the gospel to *all creation* (Mark 16:15 NASB). Because we don't know who they are, we are to preach to everyone so that those being given to Jesus hear about Him and place their faith in Him. We play a part in their salvation just as others who belong to Him play a part in ours.

God has chosen to give eternal life to those who respond to the truth about Jesus with faith. Though the Father knows ahead of time how each person will respond when they hear the truth, He doesn't decide for them what they will do. He allows each one to respond as they will.

God determined from the very beginning that those who would enjoy life with Him would do so because they choose to. He created man in His likeness with a will to choose. He decided that man, through exercising his own will, would determine whether or not he would abide with God. The Creator gave Adam the freedom to choose life or death in the Garden of Eden. As a result of Adam's choice to disobey God and eat the fruit of the forbidden tree, the condemnation of death came upon mankind. Eternal death is the judgement that man brought upon himself.

It wasn't God who condemned man. Man condemned himself through his own willful choice.

One of the more difficult questions regarding salvation has to do with young children and mentally disabled persons. If they are not able to understand and respond to the gospel, will they be lost?

I honestly don't know. Only God knows the condition of soul and faith of every person.

I do not believe a person is held eternally responsible for what he doesn't know. I believe he is held responsible for what he does know. There is something that a person, if he knows, is fully accountable to God for knowing. If and when he does know, only God Himself is able to determine and to judge accordingly.

That something is sin.

Since the fall of Adam, man has possessed the knowledge of good and evil (Genesis 3:22). He knows right and wrong. His conscience bears witness that he knows. The word "conscience" means "with knowledge". Those with knowledge of sin are accountable to God for knowing.

Through Adam, sin entered the world spreading death and condemnation to mankind. Because of his disobedience, all men were made sinners (Romans 5:12-18). The judgment of eternal death hangs over all who sin. However, because God is who He is, He took the choice that Adam made and is causing it to ultimately fulfill His desire to offer mankind His love and eternal life as He originally intended. This offer is being made through His Son who has conquered sin and death for us.

Though Adam's descendants didn't have a choice in being made sinners, they do have a choice in being saved from the consequence of sin. God is giving mankind the opportunity to exercise his will to make this choice. He is allowing mankind to freely choose Jesus to be saved.

God is no less sovereign over salvation because He allows man to choose for himself whether or not he will believe in Jesus for eternal life. And man has no less a free will because long ago God already chose those who would receive eternal life. In short, God has chosen to save all who freely choose to believe.

In saving man, God's choosing and man's choosing must come together. This can only happen one way. Jesus. In Jesus, the will of God and the will of man unite! Through choosing to believe in Jesus willingly, a person receives eternal life because this aligns with God's will to save those who do.

God is all-knowing. He knows those who will believe and works out what He desires accordingly. He has predestined these to become like His Son.

> And we know that God causes all things to work together for good to those who love God, to those who are called according to His purpose. For those whom He foreknew, He also predestined to become conformed to the image of His Son, so that He would be the firstborn among many brethren (Romans 8:29 NASB).

To "foreknow" is to "know in advance".

What did God know in advance?

God knew ahead of time those who would come to believe and love His Son when presented with the truth. In knowing, He predestined these to become like Jesus. How He works according to His foreknowledge of those who believe might always remain unknown to us. But knowing how isn't nearly as important as knowing why. I believe He intimately answers this question for each person who enters into a personal relationship with His Son. He does what He does because of love.

God loves all mankind. Yet He has chosen to save those who believe in His Son. His chosen are those who freely choose Jesus.

Why God would allow man to have any say in salvation is a mystery. I believe this is an aspect of His love that we don't fully comprehend. Perhaps in time, as we grow in understanding, the answer dawns on us. God's love for man involves giving us the freedom to choose because letting us have a choice is an expression of His love...whether we personally love Him in return or not.

Love allows for someone to choose whether it is received or not. If it doesn't, then it isn't genuine love. God's salvation for mankind is His love. It is pure and genuine. Therefore, a free will choice will always be involved in someone getting saved.

Some people have said, "Man has the freedom of choice but does not have a free will. Because of sin, his will is held captive by Satan." How is it possible to have freedom of choice if our will is not free to choose? Having a free will is what enables us to freely make a choice. Without it, we would not have any freedom to choose.

Having a "free will" doesn't mean being free from sin. It simply means having the ability to choose when facing a choice. At the moment of decision, man freely exercises his will. This is how God created man to be.

Those whom God has chosen are made known through the free will choice that each one exercises. This is why Jesus went up on a hill to address those who were following Him.

Enter through the narrow gate; for the gate is wide and the way is broad that leads to destruction, and there are many who enter through it. For the gate is small and the way is narrow that leads to life, and there are few who find it (Matthew 7:13-14 NASB).

Jesus knew that people had a choice to make. He spoke these words so that those who were His would hear the truth and choose the narrow gate that leads to life. The ones who believed Him did so.

Many heard what Jesus said. But not all heeded. Those who did were the ones God had appointed to eternal life. Those who didn't were not among His chosen. *"But you do not believe because you are not of My sheep"* (John 10:26 NASB). Many did not believe because they would not believe.

God knows those He is giving to His Son. They are the ones who willingly receive Jesus. These He has predestined to become like Christ. For this to happen, they must hear the message that will save them. Someone needs to proclaim this message so that these will hear, believe and be saved. The question is, who will go tell them?

> *Then I heard the voice of the Lord, saying, 'Whom shall I send, and who will go for Us?' Then I said, 'Here am I. Send me!'* (Isaiah 6:8 NASB).

When Isaiah heard the Lord, he responded and was willing to go. Because of this, God sent him.

We believers in Jesus are the ones who are to go tell others about Him. We are the ones because after He saves us, Jesus leaves us here on earth so that we can do exactly this.

Jesus told His disciples to "go" and "preach" (Mark 16:15). Those of us who choose not to tell others about Jesus will suffer loss because we are each responsible for what we do in Christ. Our reward from God will be according to what we did, or neglected to do, here on earth. Apathy towards the lost has consequences.

> *Now if any man builds on the foundation with gold, silver, precious stones, wood, hay, straw, each man's work will become evident; for the day will show it because it is to be revealed with fire, and the fire itself will test the quality of each man's work. If any man's work which he has built on it remains, he will receive a reward. If any man's work is burned up, he will suffer loss; but he*

himself will be saved, yet so as through fire (1
Corinthians 3:12-15 NASB).

*The fruit of the righteous is a tree of life, And he
who is wise wins souls* (Proverbs 11:30 NASB).

God's wisdom is far above any wisdom of man. He
wisely chose the foolishness of preaching to win souls to
Jesus. Why He did becomes clear as we preach. When we
share Jesus with others, He reaches into the heart of the
hearer to reveal truth. As He does, they become aware of
their sin and their need to repent. It's a mysterious work
in the heart of man that brings about eternal life.

How much God must love us to do this when we are
so undeserving.

Can someone repent and be saved after he dies?

*...It is appointed for men to die once and after this
comes judgment...* (Hebrews 9:27 NASB).

*There was a certain rich man who was clothed in
purple and fine linen and fared sumptuously every
day. But there was a certain beggar named
Lazarus, full of sores, who was laid at his
gate, desiring to be fed with the crumbs which fell
from the rich man's table. Moreover the dogs came
and licked his sores. So it was that the beggar died,
and was carried by the angels to Abraham's bosom.
The rich man also died and was buried. And being
in torment in Hades, he lifted up his eyes and saw
Abraham afar off, and Lazarus in his bosom. Then
he cried and said, 'Father Abraham, have mercy on
me, and send Lazarus that he may dip the tip of his
finger in water and cool my tongue; for I am
tormented in this flame.' But Abraham said, 'Son,
remember that in your lifetime you received your*

*good things, and likewise Lazarus evil things; but
now he is comforted and you are tormented. And
besides all this, between us and you there is a great
gulf fixed, so that those who want to pass from
here to you cannot, nor can those from there pass
to us.' Then he said, 'I beg you therefore, father,
that you would send him to my father's house, for I
have five brothers, that he may testify to them, lest
they also come to this place of torment.' Abraham
said to him, 'They have Moses and the prophets; let
them hear them.' And he said, 'No, father Abraham;
but if one goes to them from the dead, they will
repent.' But he said to him, 'If they do not hear
Moses and the prophets, neither will they be
persuaded though one rise from the dead'* (Luke
16:19-31 NKJV).

Salvation is given to those who receive by faith not by
sight. After a man dies he "sees" the consequence of his
sin, just as the rich man did in Jesus' parable in Luke 16.
Our natural mind struggles to accept this. Doesn't God
give a person another opportunity to be saved after he
dies since he then experiences the error of his way? Jesus
taught that this does not happen.

We must understand the crucial role repentance has
in someone being saved.

Jesus said, *"I have not come to call the righteous but
sinners to repentance"* (Luke 5:32 NKJV). He also said in
Luke 13:3, *"I tell you, no, but unless you repent, you will
all likewise perish."* Also in Luke 24:47 He says,
"repentance for forgiveness of sins" would be proclaimed
in His name to all the nations.

If we could be saved apart from repentance, why does
Jesus call us to repent?

The truth is we cannot be saved if we do not repent. Repenting of our sin is how we receive God's forgiveness for sin. Personal repentance leads to eternal life (Acts 11:18). If we do not repent, we will perish as Jesus said. This is hard for many to accept. Even so, it's true. Salvation involves repentance.

The rich man in Jesus' parable understood the need for repentance. While agonizing in Hades, (the place where the souls of the lost are held until the Day of Judgment) he begged Abraham to send someone from the dead to warn his brothers. He said, *"...if someone goes to them from the dead, they will repent."* But Abraham replied, *"If they do not listen to Moses and the Prophets, they will not be persuaded even if someone rises from the dead."* Though they may have had the opportunity to repent, his brothers would not do so because of unbelief.

Realize whom repentance applies to. It's to those who are alive on earth (the rich man's brothers). Though he knew about repentance, the rich man himself did not repent. He couldn't. Repentance isn't possible from those who have died. If it were, wouldn't this man have done so immediately?

Recognize what Hades cannot do. It cannot produce humility or conviction of sin. The rich man longed for relief from his torment but expressed no sorrow for the sin in his life that ultimately separated him from God. We know that sin was the cause of his eternal fate because of his admission of repentance. Repentance of sin would save his brothers from suffering the same fate. Bringing someone to repentance is the exclusive work of the Holy Spirit who convicts people of sin so that they can repent and be saved. Those who resist the Spirit through unbelief end up losing the opportunity to do so.

Jesus said, *"...you shall be My witnesses both in Jerusalem, and in all Judea and Samaria, and even to the remotest part of the earth"* (Acts 1:8 NASB). He also said, *"...repentance for forgiveness of sins would be proclaimed in His name to all the nations, beginning from Jerusalem"* (Luke 24:47 NASB). Repentance is for those who are alive on earth.

It's God's kindness in life that leads one to repent, not the judgment after death (Romans 2:2-8). If we die in our sins we perish. The time for repentance is now.

> *The time is fulfilled, and the kingdom of God is at hand; repent and believe in the gospel* (Mark 1:15 NASB).

> *...For He says, "At the acceptable time I listened to you, And on the day of salvation I helped you." Behold, now is "the acceptable time," behold, now is "the day of salvation"...* (2 Corinthians 6:2 NASB).

> *...Today if you hear His voice, do not harden your hearts...* (Hebrews 3:7 NASB).

Do any scriptures infer that everyone will eventually be reconciled to God?

> *...So that at the name of Jesus every knee will bow, of those who are in heaven and on the earth and under the earth, and that every tongue will confess that Jesus Christ is Lord, to the glory of God the Father* (Philippians 2:10-11 NASB).

> *For it was the Father's good pleasure for all the fullness to dwell in Him, and through Him to reconcile all things to Himself, having made peace through the blood of His cross...* (Colossians 1:19-23 NASB).

When all things are subjected to Him, then the Son Himself also will be subjected to the One who subjected all things to Him, so that God may be all in all (1 Corinthians 15:28 NASB).

For it is for this we labor and strive, because we have fixed our hope on the living God, who is the Savior of all men, especially of believers (1 Timothy 4:10 NASB).

The above scriptures are often used by proponents of universal salvation as evidence that all mankind is eventually saved from eternal judgment and reconciled to God. It's possible someone might get this impression at first glance. However, first impressions can be misleading.

Acknowledging *"Jesus Christ is Lord"* (Philippians 2:11) is not the same as receiving Him as Lord. What I experienced growing up has helped me to realize this.

When I was young, I attended a church which professed that Jesus was the Lord and Savior of mankind. I often knelt and prayed to Him. I even confessed my sins to a cleric in a confessional booth. For years I bowed, knelt and confessed but it never stopped me from sinning. None of these things were able to change me on the inside.

I knew about God but in reality my heart was far from Him. I needed to be taken eight thousand miles from home to a remote island in the Pacific Ocean to hear that God wanted to have a relationship with me. I was stunned. In all my years at that church no one ever told me this was God's desire. He loved me and wanted to have relationship with me personally. But sin separated me from Him. I repented of my sin and personally received Jesus as MY Savior and MY Lord. I was then baptized. On that day, my heart was completely changed. It was made new. I knew then without a doubt that I was loved and forgiven.

What is Philippians 2 saying about every knee bowing and every tongue confessing? Is all of mankind calling on the name of the Lord to be saved as some propose? Are people repenting of sin and experiencing spiritual rebirth? What is actually going on?

Let's step back and look at it in context.

> *Being found in appearance as a man, He humbled Himself by becoming obedient to the point of death, even death on the cross. For this reason also, God highly exalted Him and bestowed on Him the name which is above every name, so that at the name of Jesus every knee will bow of those who are in heaven and on earth and under the earth, and that every tongue will confess that Jesus Christ is Lord, to the glory of God the Father. So then, my beloved, just as you have always obeyed, not as in my presence only, but now much more in my absence, work out your salvation with fear and trembling; for it is God who is at work in you to will and to work for His good pleasure* (Philippians 2:8-13 NASB).

Is this passage of scripture speaking of people getting saved?

Part of the answer lies with *"those who are in heaven"*.

What need is there of repentance and spiritual rebirth for those in heaven? There is none. Those who are already with God don't need to be saved. So this must be referring to something else.

The other part of the answer can be found in the statement, *"work out your salvation with fear and trembling."* But first, I want to point out something that is often overlooked.

God is sharing something very special with us in this passage of scripture. He is telling us about His love for His Son.

Jesus poured out His life for the Father. He loved the Father so deeply that He laid down His life to fulfill the Father's desire to provide the way for man to be saved. There is no greater love than this. The depth of love between the Father and Son is immense...too immense for man to fully comprehend. The Father is letting us know, in a way we can understand, what the love and sacrifice of His Son means to Him. It means so much that He gave Jesus the name above all names. And to the Father's pleasure, all of creation, willingly or not, will bow to His exalted Son and acknowledge His Lordship. This is how much the Father loves the Son.

The exaltation of Jesus came about because He humbled Himself. We are exhorted to have the same attitude of heart and to abide in like humility. If we're not willing to humble ourselves and acknowledge the Lordship of His loved Son, God is very capable of bringing us to our knees. There's an eternity of difference between those who bow and confess out of adoration and those who do so because they are constrained to. This is why we're to *"work out our salvation with fear and trembling."*

Confession isn't always accompanied with a conviction of wrong doing and a repentant heart. I know this is true by experience.

1 Corinthians 15 tells us that Jesus will one day put all His enemies under His feet. He will then hand over the

kingdom to God so that *"God may be all in all."* Proponents of Universalism say this is proof that God's eternal life will be in everyone, therefore everyone will be saved.

This reference of Jesus subjecting His enemies comes as the apostle Paul is teaching the Corinthians about the resurrection of believers. He uses the word "all" a number of times. So let's look at this passage in context to find the meaning of "all".

> *But now Christ has been raised from the dead, the first fruits of those who are asleep. For since by a man came death, by a man also came the resurrection of the dead. For as in Adam all die, so also in Christ all will be made alive. But each in his own order: Christ the first fruits, after that those who are Christ's at His coming* (1 Corinthians 15:20-23 NASB).

All of mankind dies because all of mankind was in Adam (in seed form) when he sinned. In Adam comes death. Now look carefully at what immediately follows. *"So also in Christ all will be made alive."* Again, *"in Christ"*. Paul is making a critical distinction. He is telling us that all of those who are *in Christ* will be made alive. He's talking about the resurrection of believers! Not all of mankind will have eternal life. The resurrection of life is for *"those who are Christ's at His coming."* He is revealing an exclusive truth. Not all of mankind has part in the resurrection of life. However, every person in Christ does! Jesus is *"the resurrection and the life"* (John 11:25). All who are in Him are made alive.

In Adam is death. In Christ is life. We are born into this world dead in Adam. We need to be taken from Adam and placed in Christ to be made spiritually alive. We need to be born again.

God's righteousness in Christ does not come to us like the offense of Adam. Adam's sin was automatically imputed to all because all of mankind was in him when he fell. We didn't have a choice in the matter. God's righteousness, though offered to all, is not automatically imputed to all. Our individual will is involved. Now we have a choice. Righteousness is a gift (Romans 5:17). And as is true of any gift, it is only possessed when it is voluntarily received. It is offered to us not imposed upon us. We can accept or refuse this gift. To possess righteousness, we receive Jesus willingly by faith. When we do our guilt is removed. We are then justified in the sight of God (Romans 5:1) and no longer under the curse of Adam. We are a new creation in Christ and have become a child of God.

So the "all" here is understood. It is all of those who are in Christ.

Now, what about the "all" in *"all in all"* (1 Corinthians 15:28)?

This passage is referring to the resurrection and the time of the end. Jesus is gathering those who are His to Himself and doing away with His enemies, including physical death. He defeated death through His resurrection and is now completing the victory by raising to life the body of those who are in Him at His coming. When all things are subjected to Jesus, He then subjects Himself to the Father.

What does this passage say about the enemies of Jesus? Where are they? They are vanquished under His feet. Where are those who belong to God? They are alive with Jesus. If believers are raised to eternal life in Christ, and His enemies are vanquished to destruction under Him, wouldn't *"that God may be all in all"* refer to all those who are made alive in Christ and not those who are abolished? Remember, Jesus is abolishing His enemies and presenting only those who are in Him to the Father.

The last enemy abolished is death (1 Corinthians 15:26). So how could God's eternal life be in the death that Jesus abolishes, as Universalism implies?

It isn't.

There is another "all" that we need to take a look at. It's found in a passage of scripture that is central to the doctrine of universal salvation. This scripture is offered as proof positive that every person who has ever lived will eventually be reconciled to God.

Colossians 1:20 states that it was the Father's good pleasure for Jesus *"to reconcile all things to Himself"*. If Jesus reconciles all things, this must mean that everyone will eventually be reconciled to Him, including those who die in their sin. Right? If we focus on just this one portion of scripture and ignore the rest, it would appear as though this could be true. But let's look at it in context to understand what is actually being said.

For it was the Father's good pleasure for all the fullness to dwell in Him, and through Him to reconcile all things to Himself, having made peace through the blood of His cross; through Him, I say, whether things on earth or things in heaven. And although you were formerly alienated and hostile in mind, engaged in evil deeds, yet He has now reconciled you in His fleshly body through death, in order to present you before Him holy and blameless and beyond reproach if indeed you continue in the faith firmly established and steadfast, and not moved away from the hope of the gospel that you have heard, which was proclaimed in all creation under heaven, and of which I, Paul, was made a minister (Colossians 1:19-23 NASB).

To *"reconcile all things to Himself"* is not speaking of some future event that occurs in the coming age. It is referring to what Jesus is doing now in this present age. He is now reconciling people in this dying world.

Jesus *"made peace"* between man and God *"through the blood of His cross"*. He now has all authority in heaven and on earth to reconcile those who call upon His name throughout this present age before it comes to an end.

The gospel of Jesus is being preached throughout the world. People are believing in Him and are being saved. Jesus started His reconciling ministry when He came to earth. Just before He ascended to heaven, He placed this ministry into the hands of His disciples. He charged them to go into the entire world and preach so that He can reconcile others through them. After Jesus has saved all whom the Father has given Him, He will then subject His enemies under His feet and present to the Father those whom He has reconciled from the earth.

The reason reconciliation takes place on earth is that man's separation from God occurred on earth. It is the place where God intended man to have dominion with Him from the beginning. He is reconciling man to Himself so that man can experience and exercise the dominion God created him to have.

There is an extremely important conditional clause that Paul uses in this passage of scripture. He said, *"... if indeed you continue in the faith firmly established and steadfast..."*. If we continue in *the faith*, what Jesus did on the cross for us will present us before Him holy and blameless and without reproach. The faith Paul is referring to is faith in Jesus as Savior in which we believe the shedding of His blood removes our sin. This faith saves us. *"For by grace you have been saved THROUGH FAITH; and that not of yourselves, it is the gift of God"* (Ephesians 2:8). The grace of God which saves us comes to us through faith. If we depart from this faith and move away from the hope of the gospel that was preached, we will not have the grace to stand before Him holy or blameless. The reproach of our sin will remain upon us. The Holy Spirit inspired Paul to convey this truth so that we would understand how remaining steadfast in our faith in Christ is crucial to being saved.

This is why in his letter to Hebrew believers Paul writes, *"Take care, brethren, that there not be in any one of you an evil, unbelieving heart that falls away from the living God. But encourage one another day after day, as long as it is still called "Today," so that none of you will be hardened by the deceitfulness of sin. For we have become partakers of Christ, if we hold fast the beginning of our assurance firm until the end..."* (Hebrews 3:12-14 NASB). The beginning of being assured salvation starts with our faith in Jesus. The fulfillment of our assurance comes after we have been steadfast in faith to the end, either until our death or until He returns, whichever comes first. Paul is exhorting believers to stand fast in faith and not fall away in unbelief because this is literally an eternal life or death issue.

Jesus reconciling all things is not the same as Jesus "subjecting" all things (1 Corinthians 15:24-28). There is an eternity of difference between the two.

The reconciling that Jesus is doing now saves people from eternal destruction and unites them with God. The subjecting that Jesus does at the end of the age abolishes His enemies and puts them under His feet. His enemies will not be reconciled to Him. Only those who have been saved through the ministry of reconciliation are redeemed.

> For if while we were enemies we were reconciled to God through the death of His Son, much more, having been reconciled, we shall be saved by His life. And not only this, but we also exult in God through our Lord Jesus Christ, through whom we have now received the reconciliation (Romans 5:10-11 NASB).

There is something puzzling in the above passage. Paul says that Jesus reconciled us to God while we were His enemies. How could Jesus have reconciled us to God if He doesn't reconcile His enemies?

The answer is found in "when".

> Now all these things are from God, who reconciled us to Himself through Christ and gave us the ministry of reconciliation, namely, that God was in Christ reconciling the world to Himself, not counting their trespasses against them... (2 Corinthians 5:18-20 NASB).

When was God in Christ reconciling the world to Himself, not counting their trespasses against them?

It was, and is, during this present age.

Jesus does reconcile His enemies in this age. We who have been redeemed are living proof. In the age to come, He abolishes them. This means that we do not want to depart from this world as His enemy. God has provided a way so that we don't have to.

How could Paul first say *"we WERE reconciled to God"* and then say *"we have NOW received the reconciliation"*? Didn't we receive the reconciliation when we were reconciled?

No. This is the point that Paul is making to the Roman believers.

Before we come to faith in Jesus, we are His enemies. Our sin makes us so. However, *"while we were yet sinners, Christ died for us."* (Romans 5:8). Paul is saying that the work to reconcile mankind has been accomplished. Jesus died for us, made peace between man and God through His blood, and reconciled us to God...all while we were His enemies and dead in our sin. He completed the work that reconciles mankind. However, knowing this cannot save anyone.

There is something else we need to know. It's what separates the true gospel of salvation from all other false gospels.

It is this.

...Much more, having been reconciled, we shall be saved by His life (Romans 5:10 NASB).

Though the work to reconcile us has been accomplished, we need to possess the life of Jesus to be saved. It is His life which saves us! We must have the life of Jesus in us to be saved from the judgment of the second death that looms over mankind. It is *"...Christ in you the, hope of glory"* (Colossians 1:27). We cannot, and will not be saved any other way.

God is offering the eternal life of His Son to us now in this present age through the ministry of reconciliation. When we repent of our sin and personally receive Jesus as our Lord and Savior, through the Holy Spirit we receive His life and the reconciling work He accomplished on our behalf. In receiving His life, we receive the reconciliation!

...We also exult in God through OUR Lord Jesus Christ, through whom we have now received the reconciliation (Romans 5:11 NASB).

Believers today are the fruit of the reconciling ministry that Jesus started long ago.

If people could receive the reconciliation after they have died in their sin, the preaching of the gospel here on earth would be pointless. But they can't. This is why we who have received have also been given the charge to tell others how they can receive the reconciliation. *"Therefore, we are ambassadors for Christ, as though God were making an appeal through us; we beg you on behalf of Christ, be reconciled to God"* (2 Corinthians 5:20 NASB). God Himself, the Savior of all men, is pleading with mankind through us to believe in His Son and receive His reconciliation before it's too late.

To say that God is *"the Savior of all men"* (1 Timothy 4:10 NASB) does not mean that all men are saved. God is the Savior of all who believe whether they are a Jew or a Gentile. He's the Savior of all because *"...there is salvation in no one else; for there is no other name under heaven that has been given among men by which we must be saved"* (Acts 4:12 NASB).

Why would the apostle Peter warn, *"we must be saved"* if everyone is eventually saved in the end anyway as Universalism claims?

Why should man be warned of something he's not in danger of? If man isn't in danger of not being saved, then why is he warned to *"be saved"*?

Man is warned because those outside of Christ ARE in danger! They are in danger of destruction...the eternal death sentence. We need to be in Jesus in order to be saved from having this sentence executed upon us.

Then what does it mean that God is the Savior of all men, *"especially of believers"?*

Though God is the Savior and is certainly the one who can save all men, believers are the ones who are saved. God has chosen that salvation should come to those who receive Jesus by faith. Believers are those who have gone from being candidates of salvation to being recipients. They realize God's salvation. They believe His word, receive Jesus by faith and are then saved.

Among all the many candidates on the face of the earth, we don't know in advance who will receive salvation. It's not for us to know. We are to preach Jesus so that their candidacy can become reality. When we do, it then becomes apparent who the recipients are.

If all men are saved then Jesus was very wrong about Judas Iscariot, the man who betrayed Him. He says of Judas, the *"son of perdition"*, that he *"perished"* (John 17:12). Jesus speaks of his fate in the past tense. How could Judas have perished if he is saved?

Jesus said, *"...woe to that man by whom the Son of Man is betrayed! It would have been good for that man if he had not been born"* (Matthew 26:24 NASB).

How could not existing at all be better than salvation that Universalism claims Judas has?

Jesus is telling the truth. Judas isn't saved.

John the Baptist tells us, *"He who believes in the Son has eternal life; but he who does not obey the Son will not see life, but the wrath of God abides on him"* (John 3:36 NASB). John says unbelievers will not see eternal life. They remain under God's wrath. Universalism says unbelievers do not remain under God's wrath. They will see eternal life.

I believe John is right.

The apostle Paul wept for those who opposed the message of the cross. He realized where their unbelief would ultimately lead them. He said, *"For many walk, of whom I have told you often, and now tell you even weeping, that they are the enemies of the cross of Christ: whose end is destruction..."* (Philippians 3:19 NASB).

If they were going to ultimately be saved, I don't think Paul would have wept for those whose end is destruction.

Telling others about Jesus does come with a cost. Paul intimately understood this by experience. It's a cost that is paid through love as I hope you will see further on.

When does Jesus sum up all things in Himself?

...In all wisdom and insight He made known to us the mystery of His will, according to His kind intention which He purposed in Him with a view to an administration suitable to the fullness of the times, that is, the summing up of all things in Christ, things in the heavens and things on the earth (Ephesians 1:8-10 NASB).

...But now once at the consummation of the ages He has been manifested to put away sin by the sacrifice of Himself (Hebrews 9:26 NASB).

For while we were still helpless, at the right time Christ died for the ungodly (Romans 5:6 NASB).

God has made known to us the mystery of His will. Because He has, it is no longer a mystery. His will is *"the summing up of all things in Christ, things in the heavens and things on the earth"*. He revealed this to us when the time was fully right to do so.

If God revealed to us that this is His will, has He also told us when and how this is accomplished? Yes, He has.

Proponents of Universalism say that the summing up of all things in Christ occurs at the consummation of the ages. This is true. However, they presume that this happens in the age to come and includes Jesus reconciling those who have been cast into the lake of fire after they have been judged (Revelation 20:12-15). Therefore, everyone will be saved. Here they are in error.

When does the consummation of the ages occur?

...But now once at the consummation of the ages He has been manifested to put away sin by the sacrifice of Himself (Hebrews 9:26 NASB).

Realize what the above scripture is saying. The statement *"now once at"* means, "now having come to" or "now having arrived at". It's in the present tense. The consummation of the ages has NOW come. It began when Jesus was revealed on earth to put away sin and is still going on now in our day.

Jesus died and rose again and is now summing up all things in Himself. He is doing so by ministering reconciliation to those who believe in Him. Reconciliation occurs before the Day of Judgment, not after. The purpose of reconciliation is to reunite man with God and keep him from having the judgment of eternal destruction executed upon him. This is why God is pleading with mankind to be reconciled to Him now.

Telling others about what Jesus has done reconciles people to God. Those who believe, receive the reconciliation offered to mankind and are saved. They then begin a challenging but glorious journey of being conformed into the likeness of Jesus. It is a journey of intimacy with Him so that He can work through them to save others just as He has worked through others to save them.

It is not a mystery. Jesus is gathering out of this dying world citizens for His heavenly kingdom and is summing them up in Himself. He is transforming them into His image...the image that he intended man to have at the beginning and throughout eternity.

What does Jesus save people from?

...And to wait for His Son from heaven, whom He raised from the dead, that is Jesus, who rescues us from the wrath to come (1 Thessalonians 1:10).

He who believes in the Son has everlasting life; and he who does not believe the Son shall not see life, but the wrath of God abides on him (John 3:36 NKJV).

Serpents, brood of vipers! How can you escape the condemnation of hell? (Matthew 23:33 NKJV).

There is therefore now no condemnation to those who are in Christ Jesus... (Romans 8:1 NKJV).

These will pay the penalty of eternal destruction, away from the presence of the Lord and from the glory of His power... (2 Thessalonians 1:9 NASB).

And the smoke of their torment goes up forever and ever; they have no rest day and night, those who worship the beast and his image, and whoever receives the mark of his name (Revelation 14:11 NASB).

But the cowardly, unbelieving, abominable, murderers, sexually immoral, sorcerers, idolaters, and all liars shall have their part in the lake which burns with fire and brimstone, which is the second death (Revelation 21:8 NKJV).

Blessed and holy is the one who has a part in the first resurrection; over these the second death has no power (Revelation 20:6 NASB).

Then death and Hades were thrown into the lake of fire. This is the second death, the lake of fire. And if anyone's name was not found written in the book of life, he was thrown into the lake of fire (Revelation 20:14-15 NASB).

Most assuredly, I say to you, if anyone keeps My word he shall never see death (John 8:51 NKJV).

We know what happened in the beginning. Adam sinned, disobeyed God, and brought the judgment of death upon mankind. God's punishment for sin is man being condemned to everlasting destruction in the lake of fire. Eternal punishment is not redeeming as Universalism claims. It is condemning, which is why it's called "condemnation". It's the wrath of God against man for sin.

To escape the eternal punishment, we need to be saved!

The salvation that Jesus provides saves us from wrath and condemnation. Those who repent and trust in Him for the forgiveness of their sin take part in the resurrection of life. Over these the *"second death"* has no power. The second death is *"the lake of fire"* (Revelation 20:14). Being in Jesus saves our body from the corruption of physical death and our soul from entering eternal destruction in the second death (John 8:51).

Eternal destruction (2 Thessalonians 1:9) is not annihilation. The soul of those who fall to judgment continues to exist and experiences conscious torment in the lake of fire. In that place there is weeping and gnashing of teeth (Matthew 13:42). Its fire is unquenchable and cannot be extinguished (Matthew 3:12; Mark 9:43-48). Jesus says, *"And the smoke of their torment goes up forever and ever"* and *"they have no rest day and night"* (Revelation 14:11, 20:10). If the destruction of the soul involved annihilation, the soul would cease to exist and there would be no torment. Also, there would be no need for the fire to be unquenchable. But it is unquenchable and for a reason. Eternal destruction in the lake of fire is ongoing. The anguish experienced in judgment does not stop. This is why the soul of one who is thrown into this fire has no rest *"day and night"*.

I shudder to think of what happens to those who perish in the lake of fire.

Universalism claims the perishing of those in the lake of fire ultimately brings about their salvation. It insists perishing is "redemptive correction" that purges people of sin so that they can receive eternal life.

Is perishing redemptive? Can people be saved through perishing?

We can know with absolute certainty by answering one simple question. In fact, the answer to this question causes the doctrine of universal salvation to completely fall apart.

What is salvation?

Salvation is Jesus saving people from entering the lake of fire (Matthew 25:31-46; Luke 3:17; John 8:51; Romans 5:9; 1 Thessalonians 1:10, 5:9; Revelation 21:6-8).

Since salvation keeps people from entering the lake of fire, how can it be true of Universalism that says people can be saved by going into it?

How could perishing in the second death lead to salvation when salvation is Jesus keeping people from entering the second death where they perish?

At its core the doctrine of Universalism contradicts what is true about salvation. It denies Jesus and the way He saves people. Those who receive the love of the truth through faith in Christ are kept from perishing. These are given eternal life. Those who do not receive, perish (2 Thessalonians 2:10). They experience the condemnation of the second death.

The second death is not a place of redemption that leads to eternal life. It is a place of perishing in eternal destruction. Redemption is found only in the Redeemer Jesus. He is the way, the truth and the life. There is no death in Him. The second death is not a way to salvation. It is the very condemnation that Jesus saves us from!

God is a consuming fire (Hebrews 12:29). But He is not the lake of fire.

In Revelation chapter 21, which describes the new heaven and earth to come, we are told there will no longer be death, mourning, crying or pain. The first things have passed away. The One sitting on the throne says *"It is done."* He then immediately tells us there are those who will have part in the second death, the lake of fire, where Satan, the false prophet and the beast are in torment. So which death is being done away with? It's the death that Jesus abolishes through resurrection... physical death! This is the last enemy to God's plan of redemption for mankind. This death is thrown into the lake of fire (Revelation 20:14). The lake of fire, the second death, continues on (Revelation 21:8, 22:15).

Those who are saved are those whose names are written in the lamb's book of life. Those whose names are not in the book of life are thrown into the lake of fire. The meaning of this word "thrown" is very revealing. It means, "to throw without caring where it falls".

If everyone is universally saved from the second death, why then is the book of life even kept?

How does God's mercy triumph over judgment?

For judgment will be merciless to one who has shown no mercy; mercy triumphs over judgment (James 2:13 NASB).

What if God, although willing to demonstrate His wrath and to make His power known, endured with much patience vessels of wrath prepared for destruction? And He did so to make known the riches of His glory upon vessels of mercy, which He prepared beforehand for glory...? (Romans 9:22-23 NASB).

But when the kindness of God our Savior and His love for mankind appeared, He saved us, not on the basis of deeds which we have done in righteousness, but according to His mercy, by the washing of regeneration and renewing by the Holy Spirit, whom He poured out upon us richly through Jesus Christ our Savior (Titus 3:4-6 NASB).

It saddens me to know that there are people who will one day go to destruction. More importantly, it grieves the One who created them. For a reason that only He fully knows, He exercises patience with them so that He can make His glory known to those who receive His mercy. The Egyptian Pharaoh of Moses' day is just one example of this (Exodus 4-14, Romans 9:14-20). God used this Pharaoh, who was eventually destroyed, to show merciful deliverance to the children of Israel. We must guard ourselves from being offended at this. The potter does have a *"right over the clay to make from the same lump one vessel for honor and another for dishonor"* (Romans 9:21).

We need to be careful not to make God according to our liking. There is no moral or legal code that He is accountable to apart from Himself. He also isn't answerable to us for our dislike of eternal punishment and what it involves. It's difficult for us to understand how He can allow someone to undergo eternal destruction and be perfectly compassionate and sinless while doing so. It's also challenging to comprehend how He can do this while remaining exactly who He is...Love.

God is both Judge (Hebrews 12:23) and Father. He is Judge to those who are condemned and Father to those who are redeemed. Even as Judge, He is now mercifully calling out to people to receive pardon for sin through His Son. This is how good He is. In the cross of Jesus, mercy triumphs over judgment. We obtain God's mercy when we receive Jesus by faith before departing this earth.

God's mercy goes hand-in-hand with His love.

What is God's unfailing love for mankind?

Father, forgive them, for they do not know what they are doing (Luke 23:34 NASB).

We know love by this, that He laid down his life for us... (1 John 3:16 NASB).

Love never fails... (1 Corinthians 13:8 NASB).

Love is the motivation we're to have as believers in everything we do. This wouldn't be possible though if it wasn't for the One who showed us what love is.

"Father, forgive them, for they do not know what they are doing." This was Jesus' last earthly request of the Father as nails were being driven through His hands and feet.

What Jesus did for us is the greatest demonstration of love in all of history. Not only history, but for all eternity. The Son of God gave His life so that man can be saved. If we do not realize love through Him, we will never realize love. For there is nothing more precious to the Father, nothing more holy and perfect that He could give than the life of His Son to show us His love.

We know love because Jesus laid His life down for us.

The Father has honored Jesus' request. He is offering man forgiveness for his sin. He is telling us to repent and place our lives into the pierced hands of the One who was crucified for us. Salvation will not come any other way. No amount of torment in Hades or the lake of fire is able to produce repentance that leads to eternal life. There is only One who brings us to conviction...only One who makes us righteous...only One who redeems us. Our Savior is a person, not a place or a process. We are called to have relationship with Him to be saved.

The cross of Jesus is God's unfailing love towards man. He never fails to save anyone who comes to Him in faith. All who do are saved.

Where did the idea of universal salvation come from?

Is Universalism the gospel of Jesus or is it "a different gospel" of which the apostle Paul strongly warned against (Galatians 1:6-10)? I hope that having answered the previous important questions you can see

Universalism for what it really is. It is a doctrine filled with error.

Error leads to deception and deception ultimately leads to destruction. Man's history is proof.

Long ago Satan proudly proclaimed that he would be like God (Isaiah 14:14). In like deception, he tempted Eve saying, "You will not die...you will be like God, knowing good and evil." He lied to her. Mankind was already created in God's likeness and knew "good". But knowing evil killed them. There is only one God and only He is capable of handling the knowledge of both good and evil. From that day on, mankind has experienced death and destruction as a result of knowing evil.

Satan continues to deceive people today. Through the doctrine of universal salvation he is using the same ploy that he used against Eve. "You will not die (in the second death)...(in the lake of fire) you will become like God." It is a lie that comes from "the father of lies" (John 8:44).

Eons in the lake of fire will never produce life with God. Life, whether natural or spiritual, comes only from the Spirit of God (John 6:63). Universalism is a doctrine that was cunningly devised to deceive mankind and bring destruction upon him. Sadly, it has done exactly that.

God is mercifully offering deliverance from deception and the disastrous consequence of knowing evil. Jesus, the Savior, is God's gift of salvation to man...for those who receive Him here and now.

3

Knowing the Eternal

I'll never forget that life changing day on Okinawa back in September of 1978. Though there was much that I didn't understand at the time, this I did know. I experienced a miraculous spiritual awakening. After I was baptized in water, I was immersed into the living reality of the eternal God. Jesus changed the course of my life and gave me a new eternal destiny.

Gunnery Sergeant Truitt, and his wife Linda, drove me from the missionary church that we attended that day back to the military base where I was stationed. We rode in their little three-seat Japanese micro van that wasn't much bigger than a miniature clown car you would see at a circus. I barely fit in the back seat which put me just inches behind Gunny. I was experiencing such joy because of what God had done for me that all the way back to the base the only thing I can remember saying to them is, "I want to be like Jesus. I want to be just like Him". These words kept gushing out of me as we talked. It was a sincere and unrestrained response of my heart to being set free by the life and love of Jesus. I was so grateful for Him saving me that I wanted to be like Him.

I thought I was going to drive Gunny nuts in that little van. I just couldn't hold back the passion that God birthed inside me. Gunny looked over at Linda and smiled. She smiled too. From that time on, I've been on a life-long journey experiencing Jesus fulfill my desire.

God wants us to know Him here and now in this lifetime. He wants us to intimately experience who He is and the life He desires for us. In knowing Jesus, we know

God. When we enter into relationship with Jesus, the eternal purpose of being like Him is birthed in us by His Spirit. Our being like Him has been God's intent from the beginning. Through Jesus, what God has always desired for man miraculously becomes our desire.

God also wants us to know that there are things that mankind will experience in eternity. He has revealed these in His word. He's done so because He loves us and wants us to realize what lies ahead. What awaits us there is eternal.

Our knowing what is eternal will help us to understand the eternal judgment against man for sin and God's offer of salvation. If every person were to be saved, this judgment would have to be temporary in duration. Those embracing universal salvation claim that it is.

Let's look into God's word to know with certainty what is true of "the eternal".

I will focus on The New Testament of the Bible. Since it was originally written in Greek, I'd like to give attention to two Greek words. One is "*aion*" (noun). The other is "*aionios*" (adjective). These two words occur frequently throughout the New Testament. Proponents of universal salvation rely heavily upon these words in an effort to prove that the eternal judgment of mankind for his sin is temporary therefore everyone will eventually be saved and allowed to enter God's kingdom.

We'll look at the definition of these words and how they are used in scripture to see if this is so.

Thankfully, God's word doesn't require a theology degree to understand. It's able to explain itself in simple clarity.

To start, the word *aion* comes from a primary noun "*aei*" meaning "ever". *Aion* is defined in Strong's Greek Lexicon as a "continued duration, forever, perpetuity, world and age". *Aionios* is defined as durational, eternal, perpetual, forever and everlasting. For writing convenience I'll use the words *aion* and duration interchangeably. I will do the same with *aionios* and eternal.

AION

The word *aion* is used two ways in scripture. The following is one way.

The Duration of God's Life

...The twenty-four elders will fall down before Him who sits on the throne, and will worship Him who lives forever [aion] and ever [aion]... (Revelation 4:10 NASB).

The Duration of God's Kingdom, Power and Glory

For Yours is the kingdom and the power and the glory forever [aion] (Matthew 6:13 NASB).

The Duration of Jesus' Kingship, Honor and Glory

Now to the King eternal [aion], immortal, invisible, the only God, be honor and glory forever [aion] and ever [aion] (1 Timothy 1:17 NASB).

The Duration of Jesus' Kingdom

...He will reign over the house of Jacob forever [aion], and His kingdom will have no end (Luke 1:33 NASB).

The Duration the Son of God Dwells in God's House

The slave does not remain in the house forever [aion]; the Son does remain forever [aion] (John 8:35 NASB).

The Duration of Jesus' Constancy

Jesus Christ is the same yesterday and today and forever [aion] (Hebrews 13:8 NASB).

The Duration the Holy Spirit Abides with Believers

I will ask the Father, and He will give you another Helper, that He may be with you forever [aion] (John 14:16 NASB).

The Duration of God's Word

But the word of the Lord endures forever [aion] (1 Peter 1:25 NASB).

The Duration of Eternal Life for Doers of God's Will

The world is passing away, and also its lusts; but the one who does the will of God lives forever [aion] (1 John 2:17 NASB).

The Duration to Come

...And have tasted the good word of God and the powers of the age [aion] to come... (Hebrews 6:4-5 NASB).

The use of *aion* in the above passages clearly describes that which is eternal, everlasting, and without end.

Now let's look at the other way that *aion* used.

This World

...In whose case the god of this world [aion] has blinded the minds of the unbelieving so that they might not see the light of the gospel of the glory of Christ... (2 Corinthians 4:4 NASB).

This Present Evil Age

...Who gave Himself for our sins so that He might rescue us from this present evil age [aion]... (Galatians 1:4 NASB).

This Age of Darkness

For we do not wrestle against flesh and blood, but against principalities, against powers, against the rulers of the darkness of this age [aion]... (Ephesians 6:12 NKJV).

The Form of this World

...For the form of this world [aion] is passing away (1 Corinthians 7:31 NASB).

The End of the Age

...I am with you always, even to the end of the age [aion] (Matthew 28:20 NKJV).

The Ends of the Ages

...And they were written for our instruction, upon whom the ends of the ages [aion] have come (1 Corinthians 10:11 NASB).

The use of *aion* here undoubtedly describes that which is not eternal, not everlasting, and does have an end.

This begs an obvious question. How can the word *aion* be used for something that does not end AND something that does end? Isn't this contradictory?

Keep in mind the simplicity of truth.

Aion is used for both because each is "duration". One is endless in its existence. The other is temporary.

The age (*aion*) we are presently in is temporary. It will end. The one coming is everlasting!

The term *"forever and ever"* (*aion and aion*) in Revelation 4:10 is a termed used to describe the length of God's life. It is an emphatic description of "eternalness". It is not saying that God's life endures for an "ending duration and an ending duration" then ceases. God's life is endless. So is His kingdom. This double use of the word *aion* is very similar to the term used in the book of Genesis regarding Adam. God said that if Adam ate from the tree of life in the Garden of Eden, he would live *"o-lawm o-lawm"*, meaning "forever" (Genesis 3:22). This repeated Hebrew word means eternity.

Does the term *"aion and aion"* mean a duration that lasts for *"eternity"*? Yes. Could *"aion and aion"* be a combined use of both "ending duration" and "everlasting duration" to describe a duration that lasts forever? I believe it can because eternal God exists in both the temporal *aion* and the endless *aion*

AIONIOS

> ...*While we look not at the things which are seen, but at the things which are not seen; for the things which are seen are temporal, but the things which are not seen are eternal [aionios]* (2 Corinthians 4:18).

Very important truth is being conveyed in this passage of scripture. A contrast is being made between the temporal and the eternal.

Things that can be seen with the natural eye are temporary. The universe, the earth, and everything on the earth; these are temporal and will eventually come to an end. But the things which we don't see are eternal. They are *aionios* and will not end.

The Bible reveals that God's judgment of man for sin is eternal (*aionios*) in Hebrews 6:2, His punishment is eternal (*aionios*) in Matthew 25:46, and His redemption is eternal (*aionios*) in Hebrews 9:12. Though we don't fully see these now, they do exist. None of these exist temporarily.

Universalism claims God's judgment is temporary and redemptive in its purpose. Let's look at this claim in the light of the scriptures just mentioned.

God's judgment and redemption are both eternal. They do not end because the eternal isn't temporary. So how could judgment be temporary when it's eternal? It can't be.

Do you see the error?

If judgment were temporary, it couldn't be eternal. But it IS eternal. Scripture clearly tell us it is. And if it were redemptive, it couldn't be temporary because redemption is eternal. Universalism's assertion is proven false on two counts. Judgment is neither redemptive nor is it temporary. It is non-redemptive eternal punishment that does not end.

If necessary, read the above again to make sure you fully realize this error of Universalism.

What is true of *aionios* judgment is also true of *aionios* salvation (Hebrews 5:9). Neither one is temporary. Both come from an eternal God and are fully realized in the eternal, unending *aion*.

The following are all *aionios,* eternal and endless.

God (Romans 16:26)

God's Power (1 Timothy 6:16)

God's Glory (1 Peter 5:10)

God's Spirit (Hebrews 9:14)

Jesus' Kingdom (2 Peter 1:11)

God's Judgment (Hebrews 6:2)

God's Punishment (Matthew 25:46)

The Fire of Punishment (Matthew 18:8)

The Destruction in Judgment (2 Thessalonians 1:9)

God's Word (John 6:68)

The Gospel (Revelation 14:6)

Redemption (Hebrews 9:12)

Salvation (Hebrews 5:9)

Life in Christ (John 3:15)

A word search of the New Testament shows that *aionios* is used to describe ONLY that which is without end. It is not used to describe anything temporary in duration. *Aionios* is an adjective describing unending existence not temporary existence. The eternal doesn't stop existing (2 Corinthians 4:18).

Realize what would happen should the eternal ever become temporary.

God dies.

Jesus is no longer Jesus.

His kingdom, power and glory come to an end.

Jesus' kingship, kingdom, honor and glory ends.

The Son of God is forced to leave God's house.

The Holy Spirit abandons believers.

The word of God passes away.

Salvation is terminated.

Everlasting life ends.

Believers perish.

And all of this because of Universalism? Rest assured, the eternal will never become temporary.

The only way universal salvation of mankind can be made to appear plausible is to wrongly say the *aion* of God is "temporary in duration" and to redefine the meaning of *aionios* to include that which is "temporal". This is exactly what Universalism does.

At the risk of providing more information than is needed, I'd like to look at three passages of scripture which proponents of Universalism use to claim *aionios* does describe something temporary. Let's take a look at these to see if it really does.

> *Now to Him who is able to establish you according to my gospel and the preaching of Jesus Christ, according to the revelation of the mystery which has been kept secret for <u>long ages past</u>* (chronos aionios)*, but now is manifested, and by the Scriptures of the prophets...* (Romans 16:25-26 NASB).

> *Therefore do not be ashamed of the testimony of our Lord, nor of me His prisoner, but share with me in the sufferings for the gospel according to the power of God, who has saved us and called us with a holy calling, not according to our works, but according to His own purpose and grace which was given to us in Christ Jesus <u>before time began</u>* (chronos aionios)*, but has now been revealed by the appearing of our Savior Jesus Christ, who has abolished death and brought life and immortality to light through the gospel...* (2 Timothy 1:8-10 NKJV).

> *Paul, a bond-servant of God and an apostle of Jesus Christ, for the faith of those chosen of God and the knowledge of the truth which is according to*

godliness, in the hope of eternal life, which God, who cannot lie, promised <u>long ages ago</u> (aionios chronos), but at the proper time manifested, even His word, in the proclamation with which I was entrusted according to the commandment of God our Savior... (Titus 1:1-3 NASB).

The Greek word "chronos" used in these three passages is primarily defined as "a space of time" (Vines Expository Dictionary of New Testament Words). Those proposing Universalism say that a space of time is a finite period having a beginning and an end. Therefore the terms "eternal time" (*aionios chronos*) and "time eternal" (*chronos aionios*) are self-contradictory if *aionios* means "endless". Time cannot be endless if it is only for a specific period. Since God's word doesn't contradict itself, *aionios* must then be a word that describes something temporary...in this case, "time". *Aionios* can therefore be defined as "temporary" as well as "eternal".

God's word does not contradict itself. This is true. However, the assumption that *aionios* is describing temporary time is NOT true.

A space of time that has a known beginning and ending is temporary. But what about time that has no known beginning or end? Is it temporary? No. It isn't.

Again, remember the simplicity of truth.

What is time?

Time is a measure. That's all it is. It's a measure, but a measure of what? Time is a measure of DURATION.

Some things endure for a finite period. These are temporary. Others endure infinitely. These are eternal. "Time eternal" and "eternal time" are then defined as, "measure of duration eternal" and "eternal measure of duration". Since the eternal is infinite, they literally mean, "measure of duration infinite" and "infinite measure of duration". Both of these terms are describing infinite duration...a duration that cannot be defined or made finite. Neither one is temporary.

The measure of duration spoken of in these passages is infinite. This is confirmed by realizing what "time eternal" and "eternal time" are being associated with.

Romans 16:25 is speaking of the mystery which has been kept secret for "time eternal", *but now is manifested, and by the Scriptures and the prophets."*

2 Timothy 1:9 is speaking of God's purpose and grace which was given to us in Christ before "time eternal" and *"has now been revealed"* by the appearing of Jesus.

Titus 1:2 is speaking of eternal life that God promised in "eternal time", but has now been *"manifested"* in the proclamation with which Paul was entrusted.

It's difficult for the finite mind to fully comprehend the infinite. These scriptures were given to help us understand the infinite duration of the eternal. It's indefinable.

These three passages describe something enduring in eternity that has now been revealed to us by the Scriptures and the prophets, the appearing of Jesus, and the proclamation of the gospel.

Do you realize what's being described?

It's salvation in the eternal Son of God!!

It's all about Jesus! He is our salvation. He existed in eternity and came to earth to tell us how to be saved. He is now in eternity working through His believers to save those whom the Father is giving to Him. The measure of His duration isn't temporary and never has been. Both "time eternal" and "eternal time" accurately describe His infinite and endless duration.

The doctrine of Universalism contradicts God's word. It claims some occurrences of *aionios* in scripture describe the temporal while others describe the endless. In so doing, Universalism asserts that eternal judgment is temporary therefore all of mankind will eventually be saved. This assertion is exactly opposite to what the scriptures teach. Nowhere in the scriptures is the word *aionios* used to describe something temporary. It is only used to describe that which is endless. *Aionios* exclusively comes from the *aion* whose duration of existence is infinite and endless. *Aionios* means everlasting!

It's simply this. There are things that exist for a specific duration and then come to an end. These are not *aionios*. The word *aionios* is not used anywhere in scripture to describe these things. There are things which exist forever, infinitely, and do not end. These, and only these, are *aionios*. For these the word *aionios* is used.

When presented with this truth, some proponents of universal salvation then say that *aionios* actually means "divine" or "from God" so *aionios* is actually describing the "origin" or "divine quality" of something not necessarily the length of its existence. In doing this, they attempt to redefine the meaning of the word and ignore the truth about the eternal. The quality of endlessness is what defines the eternal!

Another error of Universalism involves the Greek word *"kolasis"*, meaning "punishment" or "torment" (Strong's Greek Lexicon). *Kolasis* comes from the word *"kolazo"* which means to "punish". *Kolazo* itself comes from the word *kolos* (dwarf) meaning to "curtail" or "chastise" or "reserve for infliction".

Universalism claims eternal punishment (*kolasis*) in the lake of fire is actually God's "divine correction" that purifies man of his sin so that he can eventually enter God's kingdom. Universalism fails to realize that whether *kolasis* is curtailment, chastisement, punishment, infliction, or even said to be "correction", it is perpetual and endless. Those who are thrown into the lake of fire experience *kolasis* that is ongoing. It is the final destination and eternal destruction of those *"whose end is destruction"* as Paul spoke of (Philippians. 3:19).

Universalism is essentially saying there is another savior...the lake of fire. What Jesus doesn't do for people before they die, the lake of fire will do afterwards. But as was covered earlier, there is no eternal life in the second death...only torment and destruction.

The following declaration sums up the true gospel of salvation and accurately depicts how the word *aionios* is used in scripture.

Eternal redemption in the eternal Redeemer saves us from eternal punishment in the eternal judgment. This is the eternal salvation that the eternal God offers mortal man. Hearing the eternal gospel and receiving the eternal King by faith during this temporal age brings eternal life. Those who believe and receive the eternal Son of God will spend eternity with the eternal Father in His eternal kingdom. Those who don't will not enter His eternal glory. They will enter eternal destruction.

Please don't misunderstand. I am not being cavalier in making this declaration. I'm very concerned about where people will spend eternity. I wrote this only to confirm the definition of *aionios*. It is everlasting, and without end.

May God help us to realize, and accept, what is true of the eternal.

4

Hearing Good News

When I first heard the truth about Jesus, I immediately received it as good news. Actually, it's the best news I have ever heard. The Son of God came to earth to personally save me and give me eternal life. But it would be some time later when I would fully realize why He had to come.

Jesus came because Adam blew it...for everyone. He brought down God's wrath upon all mankind.

The tree of life in the Garden of Eden is the first mention of eternal life for man in the Bible. Adam was given the breath of life but he didn't possess eternal life. The judgment that Adam brought upon himself prevented him from receiving it. Adam received death by forfeiting life with God through disobedience. God banished him from the garden so that he couldn't eat of the tree of life and live forever. Still, God has provided a way for man to be forgiven and receive what He offered him in the beginning.

The way is Jesus.

In Romans 5:9 we are told that Jesus' blood now justifies us and saves us from the wrath of God. If this is so, why will some people enter into judgment after they die as the Bible says? Is Jesus' blood insufficient payment for sin? Absolutely not! Those who are in Christ are now justified and declared righteous. They are forgiven of their sin and are saved from the eternal judgment. But those who are not in Him when they die are not justified or righteous. They pass away with their sin unforgiven. Because of this, they will enter into God's wrath.

Those espousing universal salvation say that God's goodness will eventually prevail over all of the evil in mankind. So if someone dies without faith in Christ, God will provide another way for that person to be saved, even if He has to use His wrath to do it. This is how good He is. God will overcome evil by saving everyone.

Universalism fails to see the obvious truth of salvation. God has already overcome evil with good!

The Son of God has already overcome all of the evil in mankind. His life, death and resurrection are proof. Being in Jesus makes one an overcomer. This is why God is offering Him to us here and now to be saved. In Him we overcome evil and the judgment for having known it. There is none greater than God's perfect, eternal Son. No one else and nothing else can provide eternal life. He alone is our salvation. If we do not have Him when we die, we will not be saved. A person will not be an overcomer when they enter God's wrath. They will be destroyed (2 Thessalonians 1:9).

Let's take a step back and look at what the doctrine of Universalism actually teaches.

- You can be saved from perishing in God's wrath by perishing in His wrath.
- You can be saved from receiving eternal judgment by receiving eternal judgment.
- You can be saved from destruction in the lake of fire by being destroyed in the lake of fire.
- Endless duration is temporary duration.

Universalism first tries to make the duration of eternal judgment temporary then tries to get "temporary judgment" to produce non-temporary life.

Do you see the contradictions within Universalism?

There is a sentiment that many who are involved with Universalism share.

"God is love. So everything He does must be done out of love. His judgment of man for sin must be an expression of His love. It must therefore be redemptive in its purpose because His love is redeeming. God would never allow someone to be punished forever in torment because it's not consistent with love. For this reason the idea of endless torment in eternal punishment is inconceivable. It violates God's loving nature."

Is this reasoning based in truth?

Scripture tells us that God, His life, His word, His love, His salvation, judgment, and punishment are all endless. They're endless whether we accept that they are or not. The truth of God is not dependent upon whether we like it or fully understand what it involves. We might prefer that eternal punishment be temporary but our preference doesn't determine what is true about it. God's word tells us what is true. Endless punishment is ongoing and an eternal reality that He warns us of.

Instead of claiming that endless punishment won't happen, shouldn't we be asking, "why would it happen?" Why would God allow someone to experience ongoing punishment?

God made man in His image. As God has a will, so does man. God didn't force Adam to obey Him. He let him choose. The eternal punishment brought upon mankind wasn't God's choosing. It was man's. It was man's willful choice that brought destruction upon himself.

There were two specific trees in the Garden of Eden...the tree of life and the tree of the knowledge of good and evil. One produced life the other produced death. God gave man a choice. He told man he could eat from any tree in the garden but he was not to eat from the tree of the knowledge of good and evil saying, *"In the day that you eat from it you will surely die."* The Eternal Creator gave man His eternal word. He was eternally serious about the consequence of disobedience and warned man accordingly. Disobedience would bring an eternal judgment upon mankind. Still, man willfully disobeyed. He chose to bring judgment upon himself. He could have eaten from the tree of life instead and would have lived forever. But he didn't. Man willingly forfeited life by choosing to reject the word of God.

In rejecting the word of God, man rejected God Himself. *"In the beginning was the Word, and the Word was with God, and the Word was God"* (John 1:1 NASB).

This is why judgment can never produce life with God as Universalism claims. Eternal judgment is the consequence of man having rejected life with Him.

Adam knew he was doing wrong when he chose to eat the forbidden fruit. He knew that God said it would bring about his death. Still, he ate it. At that moment man possessed a conscience knowing both good and evil and it killed him. He didn't physically die until later but he was spiritually dead nonetheless. From that day on, Adam's "eyes" were opened and he could only see life in God's creation from a fallen, fleshly perspective.

Why wasn't Adam cast into the lake of fire immediately after he sinned? God is perfect in Himself and certainly doesn't need man.

The Creator loved man whom He made. He didn't want man to be forever lost to destruction. So He provided a way for man to be saved from it.

Do you realize the Eternal Creator which Adam rejected in the garden is Jesus (John 1:1-3)?

The One Adam rejected would save mankind by executing man's death sentence upon HIMSELF! Jesus took the form of a man and received the punishment for our sin. He died on our behalf, paying the penalty for man's disobedience with His own life. He died so that we don't have to. When we choose to receive Him as our Savior, we are given eternal life and are saved from the pending judgment.

As He did with Adam, He is doing with us. God is letting us choose. Adam already chose death. As a result, the entire world has been judged. Now man is being given the opportunity to choose life. The Creator, Jesus, is now offering man the only way to be saved. The only way is through choosing to believe in Him. The opportunity to choose comes during our finite time on earth. It does not come at any other time or in any other way.

Just think of it. The Creator took our punishment upon Himself. There is no greater love than this!

If God wanted man to live forever from the beginning, why didn't He let Adam eat from the tree of life after eating from the tree of the knowledge of good and evil?

God loved Adam. Had Adam eaten from the tree of life in his fallen condition he would have lived forever under the consequence of knowing evil. He would never again have the opportunity to enjoy pure, intimate fellowship with God as the Creator intended. Wrath did come about because of Adam's disobedience. But God suspended it for man's sake. It was His love for man and His desire to bring man back into fellowship with Him that moved God to prevent Adam from eating of the tree.

Adam and Eve could have eaten from the tree of life instead of the tree of the knowledge of good and evil. It was freely available to them. If they had, they would have lived forever in a sinless state. But realize this. Had they done so, you and I would not be here today! Remember what Jesus said. Those in the eternal realm are like the angels. Human procreation does not exist there (Matthew 22:29-30).

God wasn't only thinking of Adam spending eternity with Him. He was also thinking of US!

How indescribably awesome is God!! His ways are so much higher than ours!!

Even though Adam fell, God has still brought many sons to glory as He intended. Throughout all generations, everyone who puts their trust in Jesus becomes a child of God and is taken into His eternal glory.

God is calling out to mankind in this dying world to believe in His Son so that man can be saved from perishing in wrath. Those who believe in Him receive everlasting life and are saved from the everlasting judgment. Those who will not believe will not share in His glory.

...For the testimony of God is this, that He has testified concerning his Son...And the testimony is this, that God has given us eternal life, and this life is in His Son. He who has the Son has the life; he who does not have the Son of God does not have the life (1 John 5:9-12 NASB).

He who believes in the Son has eternal life; but he who does not obey the Son will not see life, but the wrath of God abides on him (John 3:36 NASB).

And there is salvation in no one else... (Acts 4:12 NASB).

Is there any lingering doubt about where we find salvation? Universalism is not the good news it claims to be.

5

Falling Away

In the summer of 2010, I had the privilege of taking a road trip with my father on the famous American highway Route 66. We flew into Chicago Illinois, picked up a car in a neighboring state, and headed out on "The Mother Road" where we spent ten days having the time of our lives.

Dad and I visited all of the historic sites, museums, and greasy spoon restaurants that we could. Along the way we shared lots of stories, laughs, and even a few tears. Instead of going all the way to Los Angeles California where Route 66 ends, we decided to turn north when we got to Flagstaff Arizona so that we could see the Grand Canyon. From there we continued on through Nevada and Oregon and finally back to Washington where we started.

The Grand Canyon was undoubtedly the most scenic highlight of our trip. It's an exceptionally beautiful place. There is really nothing quite like it. Its grandeur is just awesome. But as glorious as it is, it's not as good as it was meant to be. In fact, nothing in nature that we see today is as good as was originally intended. The earth is disfigured. It's been marred because of sin. Man corrupted God's creation with his sin and forfeited the life God wanted him to have.

Just as Adam forfeited life with God when he fell away from Him in the beginning, there will be others who forfeit life with Him by falling away at the time of the end. The apostle Paul calls this falling "the apostasy" (2 Thessalonians 2:3).

The word "apostasy" means "defection from truth" or "falling away". Paul is saying that there will come a time when people who have known the truth of Jesus, and have believed in Him, will stop believing. Though they had known Jesus and had been made partakers of the Holy Spirit, they will turn away from Him (Hebrews 6:4-8; 2 Peter 2:20-22).

In his letter to Hebrew believers, Paul quotes an Old Testament prophecy that God spoke to His people after He had delivered them out of bondage in the land of Egypt. God warns them to not harden their hearts as some had done even though they personally experienced His mighty works of deliverance. God said that these had *"gone astray in their heart"* (Hebrews 3:7-11). They had turned their affection away from Him. Because of this they would not be able to enter His rest. Paul then warns his fellow believers.

> *Take care, brethren, that there not be in any one of you an evil, unbelieving heart that falls away from the living God. But encourage one another day after day, as long as it is still called "Today", so that none of you will be hardened by the deceitfulness of sin* (Hebrews 3:12-13 NASB).

As it happened in the past, there will be people in our day that personally experience God's delivering work who also will go astray in their heart. They believe for a while, perhaps even for years, but in time of temptation they fall away (Luke 8:13). By giving in to sin, their heart begins to harden against the truth of Jesus and the love He has for them. Eventually, they turn away and no longer follow Him. Because of this, they will not enter into the eternal rest that God has prepared for those who faithfully abide in Jesus to the end.

People don't turn away from God because there is a problem with the truth. There is no fault with truth. The problem lies with us. What we desire plays a big part in our eternal destiny. Jesus doesn't force us to make Him the center of our affection. To love and obey Him is something we do voluntarily, out of personal desire. As we abide in Him this way, He is the source of our eternal salvation (Hebrews 5:8-9). But *"...if we go on sinning willfully after receiving the knowledge of the truth, there no longer remains a sacrifice for sins, but a terrifying expectation of judgment..."* (Hebrews 10:26-29 NASB).

Sin can lead us away from Jesus, but only if we let it.

Those who follow Jesus rest securely in His hand. No one is able to take them from Him.

"My sheep hear My voice, and I know them, and they follow Me; and I give eternal life to them, and they will never perish; and no one will snatch them out of My hand (John 10:27-29 NASB).

If no one can be taken from Jesus, what happens with those who don't want to follow Him anymore?

People who do not want to follow Jesus any longer aren't taken from Him. They walk away from Him by choice. In doing so, they stop relating with Him who is the source of eternal life.

Why would anyone choose to walk away from Him?

Jesus tells us why.

"For where your treasure is, there your heart will be also" (Luke 12:34 NKJV).

What we value determines where our heart goes. If we no longer value Jesus and what He has done for us, what's to keep us from choosing to value something else and walking away from Him? We have a choice in appreciating Jesus. Will we continue to treasure what we have in Him, or will we turn away in choosing what the god of this world has to offer?

This God leaves to us.

Is Universalism playing a part in this end time apostasy that Paul writes about?

I believe it is.

In embracing Universalism, people are departing from the truth of Jesus. They are accepting an error filled teaching that opposes the true message of salvation. If believing the truth about how we are saved unites us with Jesus, turning away from this truth can separate us from Him.

What exactly is it that attracts people to the idea of universal salvation?

Is it the thought that no matter what someone does here on earth they can eventually make it into heaven? Or is it the notion that God wouldn't allow anyone to be endlessly punished for sin because that wouldn't be fair?

I believe what makes universal salvation appealing is that it promises people they can be saved without having to personally interact with God.

Universalism offers man salvation by way of an impersonal process. It promises him eternal life apart from having a personal relationship with Jesus. It appeals to man's selfish nature by allowing him to engage in sin without needing God to personally confront him in it.

But this isn't how people are saved.

God saves people by personally confronting them with their sin and giving them the opportunity to repent. He confronts us because He loves us. If He didn't, we would perish and never receive the life we were created to have with Him. It's a loving personal encounter with God where we're made aware of our true spiritual condition and offered exactly what we need...His acceptance.

We need His acceptance because deep within our soul we know rejection, and it hurts.

Adam sinned when he rejected God and His word. As a consequence, Adam painfully experienced rejection in his own soul when he was cast out of Eden, away from God's presence. It's perhaps the deepest pain the soul can experience. Because of sin, all have suffered rejection in some way. But no one has suffered more than Jesus.

...My God, My God. Why have you forsaken me? (Matthew 27:46 NASB).

Jesus' cry in agony is the greatest revelation of the fallen condition of mankind. He is separated from God by death because of sin.

He took it all upon Himself...our rejection, our sin, our punishment. Jesus, the sinless One, paid the price to bring us back to God. He left nothing undone. In His own words, *"It is finished"* (John 19:30). Nothing more can be done to save us. No duration in Hades or the lake of fire is able to produce relationship with God or make us acceptable to Him. Only when we are in Jesus, *"the Beloved"*, are we accepted (Ephesians 1:6).

Can we pause here for a moment?

I would like to ask you something.

Are you one who has wandered away from the truth of Jesus? Have you turned to go after things that aren't true, things that you know deep down are not what He desires for you? Are you concerned that you might have fallen away from Him? If so, there is hope.

You don't have to lose the life that God wants you to have. Jesus is looking for you. He is looking for the one who has gone astray. You are one that this book was written for.

Do you know the way back to Him?

The way is humility.

If we confess our sins, He is faithful and just to forgive us our sins and to cleanse us from all unrighteousness (1 John 1:9 NKJV).

God's love for you is deeper than you can imagine. He wants you to be with Him and fully experience what He has always desired for you. By you choosing to humble yourself and confess where you're at, He is able to graciously restore you. He is faithful and will respond to the cry of your heart.

God is not ashamed of you. He extends His grace to you without reservation. He invites you back into fellowship with Him. I pray you turn to Him with open arms and an open heart. He loves you very much.

6

The Greatest Work of All

After years of pouring over the Genesis account of creation and realizing what God did for Adam and how Adam responded to Him in return, I believe I now understand why things happened the way they did in the beginning.

God brought man into being in a perfect environment. Adam had direct personal interaction with Him and uniquely enjoyed the perfection of His handiwork. Adam experienced physical nearness with God like no other human being in history. Still, there was something missing. I believe Jesus later revealed to us what that something was.

> ...*If anyone loves Me, he will keep My word...He who does not love Me does not keep My words...* (John 14:23-24 NKJV).

What was missing was love.

Though God loved Adam and had given him everything He had made to enjoy, I believe Adam did not love Him in return. He did not have love for God within his heart that would enable him to keep the word God spoke to him. There was another creative work still needed. This work would not be recorded in the book of Genesis. Yet it would be God's greatest act of creation.

God would create love in the heart of man.

The work that God performed to bring all of creation into being was accomplished without Adam seeing how it was done...even when He created Eve. But the work to produce love would be done openly for all to see. Man must see this work for a genuine love of God to be created within him.

What is this work?

It's the cross of Jesus.

We know love by this, that He laid down His life for us... (1 John 3:16 NASB).

With outstretched arms, Jesus, our Creator, is calling out to whosoever will come to receive His love at the cross. When we believe what He did there comes from His love for us, a love for Him is miraculously generated within us. We're then able to genuinely love Him in return. This is the creative miracle of God that gives mankind eternal purpose. It is the crowning glory of His creation that reveals what we were created for...

...life in love with Him.

Just one question remains to be asked.

Are you in love with Jesus?

Made in the USA
San Bernardino, CA
27 June 2018